KINGDOM SEEKERS

KINGDOM SEEKERS

Mike Endicott

Glory to Glory Publications

© *Mike Endicott, 2009*

First published by Glory to Glory Publications 2009
All rights reserved.

Mike Endicott asserts the moral right
to be identified as the author of this work.

No part of this publication may be reproduced or
transmitted in any form or by any means, electronic
or mechanical, including photocopy, recording or any
information storage and retrieval system, without
permission in writing from the publisher.

Published in Great Britain by
Glory to Glory Publications, an imprint of Buy Research Ltd

orders and enquiries:
Glory to Glory Publications
PO Box 212
SAFFRON WALDEN
CB10 2UU UK

Scripture quotations taken from the
HOLY BIBLE, NEW INTERNATIONAL VERSION.
Copyright © 1973, 1978, 1984 by International Bible Society.
Used by permission of Hodder & Stoughton Publishers,
a member of the Hachette Livre UK Group. All rights reserved.
"NIV" is a registered trademark of International Bible Society.
UK trademark number 1448790.

Cover design by Roger Judd

ISBN 978 0 9551790 7 5

Printed in Great Britain
by Imprint Digital

Contents

Author's Preface	7
Introduction	11

PART 1 **The Way**
1.	Who Shall We Follow?	17
2.	We Are Not Yet Perfect and We Need Christ	24
3.	The Way to the Kingdom	29
4.	Looking For the Right Gateway	39
5.	The Sanctifying Road	49
6.	The Wounds of Life, the Wounds of Death	57

PART 2 **The Truth**
7.	Why is Jesus the Truth?	64
8.	Getting our Minds to Think Truthfully About God	74
9.	How to Grow in Truth, the Knowledge of God	78
10.	What Help is the Truth in the Face of Opposition?	84
11.	Truths to be Discovered Along the Way	90

PART 3 **The Life**
12.	Why is Jesus Christ Called the Life?	97
13.	Can the Life Help us to Move On?	105
14.	When Kingdom Work Seems to be Fading	110
15.	Can Life Return?	118

PART 4 **No one Comes to the Father Except....**
16.	Our Father in Heaven... Your Kingdom Come	123

"Do not be afraid, little flock, for your Father has been pleased to give you the kingdom."

Luke 12:32

AUTHOR'S PREFACE

Some years ago I encountered for the first time a devotional work of the seventeenth century, entitled *Christ: The Way, The Truth and The Life*, by The Reverend John Brown of Wamphray (d.1679). The framework of that classic piece of writing struck me as immensely helpful and thought-provoking, and I have used it as a way of structuring my own thoughts concerning some precious truths about our Lord Jesus Christ and life in his kingdom. This book is the result and, whilst it incorporates some insights from that earlier writer, it is certainly not intended to be a re-presentation of John Brown's text in an updated form. Scholars will be aware of that at once! Rather, from this study, my own personal response has emerged to the great theme of Jesus the Way, the Truth and the Life. So the reader will find here a series of reflections, and my main purpose in setting them out in this way is to lead us back to scripture to consider the immense significance of Jesus' declaration that he is the Way, the Truth and the Life. Needless to say, as with all teaching, please compare what is written in this book with the Bible, and if there is any conflict, then I urge you to hold firmly to the teaching of scripture, which alone is the authoritative written Word of God.

Finding the kingdom of God is, in a number of ways, like finding true love. When still quite a small boy, I recall, I asked my mother how I would find the girl I would marry. It was a question about true love: "When I grow up, how will I know when I have found the real thing?"

She replied, "Oh, you'll know alright!" She went on to explain, as part of her encouraging me to grow up into a social life of my own apart from my parents, that true love would never be found sitting on my bed, reading boys' adventure stories. It would be waiting for me somewhere out there on the road.

Of course the kingdom, like true love, looks and feels slightly different to everyone, so that to explain what it actually feels like to live there might only be misleading to others who have not yet looked for it. However, we can all begin with the understanding that living in the kingdom of God is not a matter of suddenly discovering that everything goes the right way for us from then on, but of righteousness, peace and joy in the Holy Spirit. The benefits of living there do not come in the form of gifts and talents alone, or any secular advantage at all, but in the increase of love, joy, peace, patience, kindness, goodness, faithfulness, gentleness and self-control in the kingdom seeker. (See Galatians 5:22f.) This is the most desirable place to be.

The benefits of kingdom living are numerous but may be described in two broad areas: temporal and eternal. All temporal benefits will include the eternal as, for the Christian, eternity begins to become reality on passing through what I will refer to as the gate of justification. The temporal ones, however, have already been mentioned and will grow in their intensity as the kingdom seeker progresses towards the heart of the kingdom. At its centre is Calvary with its grace. On arrival at the kingdom gate of justification, the punishment due to us has been exhausted on the cross. (See Ephesians 2:13f.) It is a place that must be reached before the seeker can be in the position described in Galatians 2:20, *I have been crucified with Christ and I no longer live, but Christ lives in me. The life I live in the body, I live by faith in the Son of God, who loved me and gave himself for me.* Christ now lives in the seeker (who is by now a repentant believer), and his ministry is: Christ doing the work in him. (See John 14:10.) The miracles the seeker works are the signs and the wonders of that kingdom in which he is now living. The prophetic gifts then flow increasingly.

Secondly, through this wonderful grace and generosity, the way becomes open for poverty of many kinds to be exchanged for God's riches. (See Deuteronomy 28:47,48; 2 Corinthians 8:9 and 2 Corinthians 9:8.)

Thirdly, perhaps the best known gift, through Jesus our mortality can be exchanged for a share in his immortality at the gate of justification. (See Hebrews 2:9)

Fourthly, we have been offered his righteousness in exchange for our own efforts to be holy. (See Romans 6:6.) The only righteousness acceptable before God is the righteousness of Christ. He gives new birth to those who come to him in repentance and faith in him. Jesus becomes our Lord and Saviour and the seeker is clothed with Christ.

Lastly, our sicknesses and pains, the things that sadden and bring sorrow, have been taken on the cross so that we might receive healing through Christ's wounds. (See Isaiah 53:5.) Jesus' words signified that this would happen. Kingdom seekers would be able to do the same work in abundance. Jesus said in John 14:12, *"I tell you the truth, anyone who has faith in me will do what I have been doing. He will do even greater things than these, because I am going to the Father."* This is not to say that the kingdom is a place full of people who can instantly receive healing, but a place full of a crucified Christ through whom healing in body, mind and spirit has already been given.

What we might call the kingdom of Christ is not somewhere that the kingdom seeker can come across by accident, nor a place to be discovered by his own unaided efforts. Neither is there any 'religious trick' that will turn the lock in the door. We are not called to find the kingdom but to seek it. It is in the seeking, rather than in the finding, where we begin to discover the knowledge and benefits of kingdom living. The nature of this holy life is revealed to kingdom seekers through their asking; they will only find it by diligently seeking for it, and the door will be opened to those who knock. But does this apply to everyone? Which of us will be able to see the kingdom? Anyone who will receive the kingdom of God like a little child, the poor in spirit and the pure in heart, can enter it, but we must have some help in starting; we must have a clue to set us on the right path, and it is this. Jesus said, *"Follow me,"* and *"I am the way, the truth and the life."* Forms and shapes of Christianity, different churches and different denominations that require little from disciples, do not count for much outside their membership. This journey into the kingdom is going to need at least as much concentration, training and perseverance as does learning to play a musical instrument. Nobody has ever drifted into a genuine kingdom experience.

The first step, and often the most difficult one for the Christian to take, is to get our lives centred on Christ. Broadly speaking, we have become acclimatised either to a relatively distant and non-intervening God or we are focused on the Holy Spirit's gifts for their own sake and his power to change lives. Instead of either of these approaches, following Christ closely along the narrow path where he leads us can only be achieved if we hold him tightly in focus in front of us, throwing all other understandings and images aside and concentrating purely on him. My hope is that this book will teach us how to do it. So I know there is much in what follows to argue over, and that many may find fault with it, perhaps with good reason. Some readers might find it arrogant of me, or at least over-confident, to attempt to handle the business of seeking the kingdom, such a mysterious, and yet essential, part of the practice of Christianity. I can only ask for open hearts to attempt the journey with me. I hope that the kingdom we find — as we find ourselves at the feet of the true Christ together, and as we follow him alone — will not be one of merely theoretical interest but of actual experience.

INTRODUCTION

It is thought by many that the kingdom of God and the church are one and the same, but they are not. In one sense, the word 'church' means the company of all faithful believers who are members of the body of Christ — those who repent, believe and go on believing in Jesus as Saviour and Lord, abiding in him. Perhaps confusingly for some, the same word 'church' is also used of many denominational organizations. The church was firstly intended to be a gathering of Christian believers for prayer, worship, teaching and mutual support, as we see happening in the Acts of the Apostles. For the purposes of this book, church might be thought of as being the spyglass through which something of the kingdom may be perceived by outsiders. It is always to be hoped that the life of the church will be open to, guided and empowered by the Holy Spirit — and true believers do experience his activity, his presence and his gifts, and want to bear the fruit of the Spirit — but history has seen many of the visible institutions falling short of obedience to Christ, and so missing much of the life of the kingdom. In the business of managing itself organisationally, in its politics, its public face, and the matching of its policies and rituals to the world, the matter of the kingdom of God has often been obscured or ignored. Not only institutions, individual Christians too sometimes lose sight of the kingdom, and Jesus' teaching about it and demonstration of its life.

Many faithful Christians have become more and more disillusioned with organised denominational activity, and they are also finding within themselves a deeper longing to see the things of the kingdom returned to church life. We discover in scripture the Lord's own will for his church. We have his mandate in the great commission, and we are to go on making disciples, who will live in his kingdom. The church constantly needs to be revived, mobilised and growing into the kind of church that he came to bring to birth. If we could set out to discover and dwell in the kingdom, we might find the church becoming a very different place, a place full of the good news of Christ and of his kingdom that changes lives for those who come near to it.

We cannot expect our understanding of the kingdom of God to be demarcated at the outset by the contours of well thought out conclusions and logical deductions! If we are determined to begin our journey to seek the kingdom of God by clambering over obstacles, having to prove its existence and benefits, we will never get started.

Our journey into the kingdom will be a question of action. If we keep stopping to find proof for everything, we will never get to the point of doing anything. To act we must make assumptions, and those assumptions are to be based on God's self-revelation in his written Word, the work of the Holy Spirit, our repentance, and our active belief and trust in the crucified and risen Lord Jesus.

So where do we look to find this kingdom? Wherever the character and will of Christ reign supreme! If we look for the kingdom everywhere, we are sure to find Christ in the midst of many situations.

On this journey the kingdom seeker becomes increasingly aware of living in a place where 'Love and faithfulness meet together; righteousness and peace kiss each other. Faithfulness springs forth from the earth, and righteousness looks down from heaven' (Psalm 85:10f).

This is how the kingdom seeker lives his or her life surrounded by the kingdom. We become wholly centred on the King. By uniting like this with him in our heart, will and spirit, we are united to all that he is and has in himself. This is the holiness and perfection of living that we pray for in the Lord's Prayer —that God's kingdom may come and his will be done in us, as it is in heaven.

This is a discoverable place of reality. If it were not so, our Saviour would hardly have made it a part of our daily prayer.

The kingdom will not, however, be found where the seeker determines it by force of his own will, but where he surrenders to the divine will. The kingdom of heaven will not surround us even when we make God's will into our law of life; the seeker will have to take a step even further than that. It will be fully around us when God's will and our will are the same.

We must begin the journey by asking the simple question: Why does God not sovereignly spread his kingdom throughout the whole world —why does he wait? Why not save us all the work of searching for it? After all, God's power is not limited by anything outside his own creative and restoring purpose.

He is, of course, all powerful, but he exercises his power as our Father. We are encouraged to pray, "Your kingdom come", and that divinely taught prayer begins with our calling to "Our Father". God's revealed nature is perfect goodness, justice and mercy. So from a position of repentance and faith we understand the omnipotence of God within the context of his Fatherly love. He does not force his kingdom on the world, but it is his good pleasure to give it to those of his children who humbly seek it. We can see something analogous to this in the measure of freedom we are given. At least for a time, if we want to, we can frustrate his plans and break his laws. On the other hand, we can freely give him our lives and the devotion of our hearts and minds, being boisterous children all in a clamour at his family table. (See Matthew 11:12.) Kingdom seekers are drawn together by the compulsive attraction of his love, not by the exercise of his might nor as a result of any ecclesiastical procedure.

It is my hope that true light dawning, by the inspiration of the Holy Spirit rather than directly from the words written here, will set other Christians on the real exercise of seeking kingdom godliness, and the daily practice of the absolutely fundamental kingdom work of living by faith and trust in Jesus Christ. The soul that travels this way and exercises itself in kingdom living will find enough work to keep it fully occupied. It will find solid ground to stand on, a solid, heart-quietening ground of peace.

What, when we find it, is the kingdom of God? The revelation that the Lord Jesus Christ himself is the chief cornerstone, and that in him the whole building is joined together and rises to become a holy temple; and that in him we too are being built together to become a dwelling in which God lives by his Spirit — such realizations as these, by definition, ought to be the most important life considerations for all of us. It is only sitting at the feet of Christ, listening to him, that we can be built up and built onto this cornerstone, to make a home where God can live through his Spirit; so studying the King and his kingdom, obeying him, abiding in him, ought to be the main work and occupation of those of us who would want to be considered by God to be faithful labourers and co-workers with him. In doing this, we would be following the apostle Paul's example in being determined not to know anything while he was among the churches he wrote to, except Jesus Christ and him crucified. (See 1 Corinthians 2:2). This great theme, Jesus Christ and him crucified, is such a soul-fulfilling heart's delight simply because it is the signpost that points directly to the centre of the kingdom. The phrase holds out to us such a tempting and tasty glimpse of the promise of that unarguably great mystery which is Christ himself, God manifest in the flesh, ministered to by angels, his truths preached to Gentiles, believed on in the world and received up into glory. Amazingly enough, *Even angels long to look into these things* (1 Peter 1:12). Some day, hopefully, the study of such things will be as much a part of churchmanship as worship, mission and financial support are today. Of course the church of Jesus Christ must be more than merely a studying church, but it cannot be anything less than a studying church and still be faithful to its Lord.

The search for the kingdom, and the study of the King at its centre, as long as it is for the purpose of obediently living our lives in it, is vital. Although Christ crucified may be a stumbling block to Jews and foolishness to Gentiles, he is the power of God and the wisdom of God to those whom God has called. The foolishness of God is wiser than man's wisdom, and the weakness of God is stronger than man's strength. (See 1 Corinthians 1:23, 25.)

The seeker will find that there are bottomless depths of the wisdom of God in this mystery of the kingdom of the crucified King!

So how do we seek the kingdom? In which direction do we set out to find it? Happily, we have the answer already written down for us, as the disciples asked the same question of Jesus. He replied that he himself was the way, the truth and the life. This is one of those sayings from scripture that seem light and airy, like a delicate summer swift that flicks past high in the sky: a delight to see and to hear, but in one breath it seems as though it is at the other end of our horizon. I set out to write this book about that very saying.

To seek the kingdom we must learn again to follow him on the most absorbing, exhilarating and life-enhancing journey of them all.

Part One
THE WAY

1

WHO SHALL WE FOLLOW?

It is always a useful thing, if not utterly essential, for we children of God to know the right way to take full advantage of our inheritance, the richness of his Son's kingdom. Christ has made provision for us, for the sanctifying journey deeper into his kingdom: *wisdom from God — that is, our righteousness, holiness and redemption* (1 Corinthians 1:30).

In fact it has never been more necessary for believers to be clear and distinct about their understanding of kingdom matters, especially in these days when Satan is looking to distort, by any means that come to hand, any right understanding of the King and his kingdom. One way or another, he is working to lead souls away from finding the true kingdom, drawing them away from the Lord Jesus Christ who is revealed in the New Testament. Our spiritual enemy obscures our vision by overshadowing the way to the kingdom with error, sometimes subtle and sometimes obvious, and by hiding it under a layer of human mistakes and prejudices. So not only are both newly arrived and growing kingdom seekers sometimes led astray, wandering off the path, but many of God's own long-established people are often walking in the darkness of ignorance and misunderstanding. Their souls and bodies remain under-nourished through a lack of real exercise of the life in the kingdom, which would make them strong, well-nurtured and flourishing, *being strengthened with all power according to his glorious might so that you may have great endurance and patience* (Colossians 1:11).

Re-focusing our life's aim on seeking the road to the kingdom is very topical. Satan has often tempted Christians into moral mistakes and emptiness. In tumbling after such temptations, the church sometimes follows the world, coming to a place of accepting the unacceptable, disobedience to God's will, as being 'normal'. And Satan seeks to direct us to accept something which is not Christ, and to rest on something which is man-made instead.

Our subtle adversary is now setting men to work in preaching, speaking and writing about a 'Christ' who is not the true Lord Jesus Christ, crucified, risen, ascended, but one built out of their own experiences of the Christian life rather than from the diligent study of scripture.

If we can so easily find the wrong Christ, then it will be easy to learn the wrong kingdom and the wrong salvation. The devil is trying to attach our souls to the wrong leader and then, finding themselves swimming in a muddy pool of ineffectual religiosity, teachers may promote a kind of morality, civility, and outward semblance of holiness, in which the soul is supposed to feel comfortable — ineffective, but at least at home.

But there were always going to be terrible times in the last days. *People will be lovers of themselves, lovers of money, boastful, proud, abusive, disobedient to their parents, ungrateful, unholy, without love, unforgiving, slanderous, without self-control, brutal, not lovers of the good, treacherous, rash, conceited, lovers of pleasure rather than lovers of God — having a form of godliness but denying its power* (2 Timothy 3:1–5).

Much of Christianity nowadays, despite a good deal of talk of a miraculous kingdom, has little or no power to cause movement in changing individual lives or in moulding society as a whole. This is because, so often, an unreal picture of Christ has been taught, a long way from the real Jesus Christ depicted in the New Testament — who overflows with mercy and grace toward all who come to him in repentance, believing and trusting in him — and who will return to judge all mankind with justice, and who will rule the world. The false 'Christ' depicted in so much wrong teaching – one who does not hear our prayer – is a mirage. An erroneous way of thinking allows the children of God to think of him as one who hangs back from his people, one who delays in bringing grace, and hides the reason for his supposed 'reluctance' from his people while we supposedly gain strength in our suffering. But the true Lord Jesus Christ, the only true reflection of the Father, is the one revealed in scripture. It is worth repeating that if we cannot see the right King we cannot see the right kingdom.

Through the great goodness of God, the truth about these things can be satisfactorily cleared up; and many Christians have, at least in theory, heard that truth. On the other hand, many gracious souls profess their unfamiliarity with the more solid and supportive ways of the real Lord Jesus Christ and of kingdom blessings that are his gift to us.

But we should not worry. God says, *"I will lead the blind by ways they have not known, along unfamiliar paths I will guide them; I will turn the darkness into light before them and make the rough places smooth. These are the things I will do; I will not forsake them"* (Isaiah 42:16). Along this glorious way we will find that Jesus Christ really is the Way, the Truth, and the Life.

So we begin by knowing that, if we really want to lead a life centred on the true Christ and immersed in his kingdom, our Lord Jesus lays down a solid path for us to walk on to get there. He strengthened his first disciples on the way when he appeared to them after his death on the cross. He encouraged them as they faced their concerns about all that might befall them when he, their Lord and Master, was taken from them. All that encouragement can be taken by us as sufficient proof of the wonderfully tender heart of Jesus, who freely gives out strengthening gifts of support and healing relief to all his followers in the face of every fear, difficulty and danger which we meet along our way.

He will not leave us without comfort, and for that reason he lays down this firm path under foot to support our drooping hearts. His support is given so that the kingdom seeker can rejoice along the way, and so that the world may see and be convinced of the reality that he (the kingdom seeker) finds in true Christianity.

The ordinary group of worshipping Christians, at least as the preacher views things from his observation platform in the pulpit, does not look to him like a collection of very joyful people! In fact, we too often look rather like a group of sad, tired and depressed people! Of course it is difficult to imagine that such people would ever win the world for Christ. It is no use trying to imagine otherwise; we may talk about joy and teach about it, but, unless we really have the joy of Christ in our hearts and really manifest it, our words will carry no conviction to our hearers.

The opposite is true as well. If we really become buried in Christ and in his kingdom so that we become his joy, then the whole world will soon know about it. The joyful Christian witnesses to the world about his preference for kingdom living, irrespective of all the troubles that might go along with this earthly life.

Jesus encouraged his disciples by telling them that they knew where he was going and the route he was taking. (See John 14:4) That was the way he intended to bring them to the Father, into eternal life, and to the mansions already prepared for them. (See John 11:16, 20:25.) But Thomas, as hasty and indecisive as often he was, allowed his unconsidered thinking to burst on the scene and almost contradicted his Master, saying, *"Lord, we don't know where you are going, so how can we know the way?"* (14:5). This may be a banner over many of us who might lack the vocabulary to express our heavenward desires, or who long for the basic truths of the kingdom to be reinstated in the foundations of our souls. Christ, as he often did, took the opportunity to clear up that area of indecision, letting his disciples see the true way of coming to the Father. He does not do this with a set of cold, hyper-intellectual observations, which might well have left them feeling inadequate and foolish. They are helped to see they were not such strangers to the way as they might at first have thought. The way Jesus reveals is perfect, fulfilling, safe, saving and satisfying, and there is a duty to be always walking further and deeper along this way, until we come home at last to the Father. Jesus says to them, *"I am the way and the truth and the life. No one comes to the Father except through me."* (John 14:6). So now the way is revealed. The way is Jesus himself.

As well as learning that he is the route to the Father, we see that he is also truth itself, and the living way, and that he is life itself. With this one expression he invites us to consider how he might be, at one and the same time, the Truth and the Life, as well as the Way. Not only that, he is the absolutely perfect, exquisitely excellent, incomparably preferable and fully satisfying way for every kingdom seeker on all occasions: in all times of trouble, all distress, all sickness, all difficulty, all times of trial, all doubts and all temptation which the Christian might meet on the way through this life to heaven.

Before we look more closely at those words — 'way', 'truth' and 'life' – we can explore several delightful points of doctrine in the preceding verse, where Thomas almost contradicted what Christ had said. Firstly, we can see from the passage that Jesus Christ has the most tender of feelings towards his followers, and will not dispense with our services, or discard us on every occasion that we might provoke him to anger or whenever we grieve his Spirit. Instead, his method is to pass gently and gracefully over many of our failings, if we are not being deliberately obstinate or rebellious. We can reach this conclusion because he knows how frail we are by nature and, having a tender heart, will not break the bruised reed (see Isaiah 43:3), knowing as he does that rough handling would crush us, and break us all into pieces. His heart is overflowing with boundless mercy, which attribute signifies compassion on those who have lost the way: *for we do not have a high priest who is unable to sympathize with our weaknesses, but we have one who has been tempted in every way, just as we are —yet was without sin* (Hebrews 4:15). These truths on their own should be enough to persuade anyone to look to him.

Secondly, we learn the lesson from the account of Thomas that weakness of soul and corruptness of thinking, when honestly and innocently brought into the open before the Lord, will not drive him away. He will still give us his help and support. A great deal of Thomas's weakness and corruption of view came to the surface in what he said, and yet it was honestly and innocently laid open to Christ, not out of a spirit of contradiction but with a longing to learn.

Thirdly, Jesus is not in any way hasty, rash or proud; but he is gentle, loving, tender and full of compassion.

Fourthly, we can see from this episode that it is part of Jesus' office and work to be an instructor to the uninformed. Would we not all willingly give ourselves over to such a teacher as this, one who will not push us towards the exit door, nor even merely leave us alone, when we think that he most likely would out of sheer frustration with us? He is patient with us.

We can now see that all our ignorance and innocent naivety, when it is honestly acknowledged and laid open before Christ, only serves to put us in the right place to learn more. Part of Christ's work is to teach the unaware, to open the eyes of the blind. It follows then that it must be the height of silliness to think we can conceal our ignorance from him, and to hide our situations and conditions from him. This should commend his grace to us even more! How happy is the person who has given up everything to follow him! Even our worst condition can now be turned to our advantage. Awareness of our own ignorance, riddled as it may be with sin, should encourage us to turn to him who will help us and increase our knowledge. Bless him for this. With joy and satisfaction, let us dwell under his teaching and his moulding.

It is remarkable how the disciples so often disclosed so many of their worldly ideas about Christ's kingdom, which turn out to be like the way many feel today about churchgoing. They seem to have understood his kingdom to be something earthly, outward, pompous, stately; and — by virtue of these features — to be a desirable condition.

We might then easily assume that there might be some of this worldly apprehension lurking behind Thomas's question, but the Lord, who knew their thoughts, wisely draws them away from such notions. He starts them off in another direction altogether, the study of the route to the Father and to the kingdom. We are shown again that *seeking* is blessed.

The very act of walking this road towards the kingdom provides substantial food for the soul. The study of this particular subject is always edifying. The fruit of this study, as it is put into practice, will most certainly be extremely profitable and long lasting for the reader.

2

WE ARE NOT YET PERFECT AND WE NEED CHRIST

If we are to follow Christ into his kingdom and live there, we do well to look again at these key words: Jesus asserts that he is the way, the truth and the life, and that no one comes to the Father except through him. If we do not learn certain things from these words, we will not sense any need for a Saviour and so may fail to realise the need to search for him and his kingdom. We may lead an active religious life, but without this foundation it will be worth little.

At the outset, we affirm that mankind is biased towards sin and is in that miserable state by nature. By 'biased towards sin' we do not mean that a person necessarily looks after himself before anyone else, or continuously commits great evil deeds, or feels hard done by in fruitless searching for worldly goods or self-satisfaction in a life constantly compared to other people's, but that he lacks a right relationship with God.

It is far easier for him to believe, if indeed he has ever thought about it, that he has reached this state of being biased towards sin through nurture rather than through nature. He can more easily accept the cause of his state to be the corrosive effect of life's experiences and upbringing, but in doing this he misses the whole basis for his need for Christ. How do we reach that conclusion? This is a hard thought which is vital, nevertheless, for our finding the right gate into the kingdom. Since Adam's first act of disobedience, all mankind is born in a natural state of alienation from God, and without true repentance and faith goes on, throughout life, living at a distance from God. It is easy enough for us to own up to some sort of general public godlessness; under cover of it, we would escape hearing any personal prompting from God. It may be better and safer, then, if we concern ourselves here with individual badness rather than of universal malignancy. By individual badness, we mean our own. We find it out in ourselves; or rather, he finds it out in us, ...*for the LORD searches every heart and understands every motive behind the thoughts* (1 Chronicles 28:9). In this context it is always better to acknowledge repeatedly before God our propensity to be natural wanderers from his presence rather than search out and compare individual acts of sin. The seeker should find, as he journeys further into the kingdom, that the degrees of shame and disgust he begins to feel at the sight of his own sins will not correspond at all with what intelligent reason says about their comparative seriousness.

This individual sense of separation from God implies our recognising that there is an ordered existence from which we have broken loose, a divine image to which our individual character is not conforming as it should. It is this character of Christ which is the true human character as it should be, and growing into it ought to be the universal objective of the whole of mankind.

We are naturally wandering creatures, blind and yet always enthusiastically ready to explore any wrongly signposted highways and by-ways without knowing where they could lead us. We are naturally incapable of discerning the true way, being blinded with intolerance and bigotry, and full of misconceptions about life, both earthly and eternal. Frankly, we are born prone to error, and unless we are given a new life we will remain that way. In our natural state we are to all intents and purposes, dead. We have no way of getting home. We cannot walk in the right direction even when someone else points it out to us. We turn our backs on the gospel whenever we hear it. Even when we do start out in the right direction we are always tethered by the guide ropes of temptation and good intention, pressing and pulling us to wander off the path, to climb over the fence and lie down where the grass seems greener and to sleep on the side of the road. It is our propensity to do such things that keeps us captive. Unless we are given new life we will die eternally.

So our natural state is utterly depressing. To see it is to grieve for ourselves and one another. Now, before we go any further with this, we affirm that kingdom seekers must be fully prepared to accept this natural and general state of mankind's affairs as a description of themselves, or there will be no way to move forward and make proper use of the blessings of Christ and his kingdom. *"It is not the healthy who need a doctor, but the sick. I have not come to call the righteous, but sinners"* (Mark 2:17). Unless we admit that we are sick we will never call for the doctor. We kingdom seekers are to live with this in mind, never forgetting how frail we are.

Although there might be real events and changes blessing our lives by the grace of God every day, we are not yet perfect, and will need Jesus Christ always to be the way, the truth and the life even until he brings us in and sets us down with him in glory. We must never set out to walk on foot without him leading us by the hand —or, rather, carrying us in his arms. All of us who would travel his way should remember what we were, and what we are, and keep a sense of our own frailty and natural state of disobedience. Following conversion and new birth there is still the battle between flesh and spirit, as the epistles show us so clearly. So it is only in this frame of mind that we can keep a good eye open for Jesus our Lord and Master, along the way, and benefit from his royal friendship and the blessings that spill from the nearness of the kingdom.

We should learn that Jesus Christ is the all-accomplishing

Mediator, perfect for all our needs and necessities. If we feel ourselves to be at a distance from the Father, then Jesus is the way to bring us together. If we have wandered out of the way, then he is the road map back for us. When we are blind and ignorant, he is the truth. When we are dead, he is the life. It is only when walking with him in the kingdom that we learn these things:

1. Jesus possesses everything that we will ever need —the way, the truth, and the life. *"The Spirit of the Sovereign LORD is on me, because the LORD has anointed me to preach good news to the poor. He has sent me to bind up the brokenhearted, to proclaim freedom for the captives and release from darkness for the prisoners"* (Isaiah 61:1).

2. He is most suitably and completely qualified to be the one and only Mediator between us and the Father. Not only does he have enough fullness, so that whatever we need is there in him, but it is also a fact that this wide-ranging fullness answers every major question in life. Have we lost our way? He is the way. Are we dead? He is life.

3. He (and therefore his kingdom) is richly full of practical and restoring benefits, for he is the one, *in whom are hidden all the treasures of wisdom and knowledge* (Colossians 2:3). *For in Christ all the fullness of the Deity lives in bodily form* (Colossians 2:9).

4. This journey to find the kingdom turns out to be a fascinating task of growth and up-building, for we are said to have been given fullness in Christ, who is the head over every power and authority (see Colossians 2:10), and we are, *his body, the fullness of him who fills everything in every way* (Ephesians 1:23).

5. We can also find here in the kingdom a satisfying sense of completeness as human beings. When we are not on the road to finding the kingdom we are rarely satisfied with life —we need to see more money or more promotion, finer possessions, more people on the pews in church or more duties and responsibilities in which to be needed by our fellows or which give us satisfaction

in the doing. However we walk through worldly life, we still cry out, 'Give me more, give me more!'

On the other hand, when we find and enter the kingdom and obtain Christ we become full to overflowing. We can only sit down with our head in our hands and cry, 'Enough, enough!' and no wonder. We have everything. We can no longer feel any strong desire for other things in the same way. We cannot seek them any more. After all, what can the person possibly want who is complete in Christ?

How different this is from any reccurring bias towards sin; how happy and contented are the seekers who find the kingdom! It is so much easier for them to counter all Satan's objections because, although they continue to live in the world, they do not wage war as the world does. The weapons we fight with are not the weapons of the world. On the contrary, they have divine power to demolish strongholds. *We demolish arguments and every pretension that sets itself up against the knowledge of God, and we take captive every thought to make it obedient to Christ.* (2 Corinthians 10:4f.).

On the other hand, consider the struggles and the emptiness of those who are strangers to Jesus. How can their needs be met? How can they confidently rise to meet and overcome all those everyday challenges, accusations, temptations, objections, doubts, fears and discouragements?

Such thoughts and promises should deeply encourage any Christian to follow the way of the kingdom and to go on believing the King at its heart. Here is the most precious treasure, worth the seeking. It is quite amazing that such an all-sufficient Saviour and Mediator, able to save and to heal everyone who comes to him, should be so under-rated by so many, so doubted, disregarded and ignored!

3

THE WAY TO THE KINGDOM

So we have recognised that we need a route map to find the kingdom and that we need a leader to take us there. We come now to look in some detail at his words, and first of all at his being *the way*. The aim here is to show how we can make use of everything that Jesus Christ offers his followers — the benefits of kingdom living in all those necessities, strains, stresses and difficulties which seem to lie like hurdles across our paths — and, in doing so, live by faith in him, grow up in him, walk in him, advance and march forwards towards glory in him.

This discussion, which concerns the full indwelling of Christ, will be quite as appropriate for the unbeliever, if that is what the reader is. It will help him to start out on the right road. And it might help to set the record right for many a believer who has been led by others to think that he is on the right highway to the kingdom when he might very well not be. Having said that, there is a joy which is not given to the unbeliever, but to those who love our Father in heaven, for his own sake. It comes to them as they pass through the gate to the kingdom, becoming his adopted children, and making life on this earth truly happy as they rejoice towards him, because of him, and on his behalf in the world.

Before we can resolve the question of how anyone can come near the kingdom and begin to enjoy the benefits of living in it, we must first be in a position to recognise our basic need for the King. We should also think about his being able to deal with our individual situation — fully, richly, and satisfyingly. This will make the way in which we might make use of the benefits of kingdom living less vague.

When Christ says 'I am the way' he implies a number of things to us. Mankind as a whole, as a species, is alienated from the Lord, and lives a nomadic life, always at a distance from him. We have left the presence of God, each one of us being a one-man or one-woman walking revolution. *All have turned away, they have together become worthless; there is no one who does good, not even one* (Romans 3:12). *Even from birth the wicked go astray; from the womb they are wayward and speak lies* (Psalm 58:3). Not only have we gone astray but we love to wander away from God. The scriptures contain many reproaches for this human tendency. We are like those being spoken about in Job 21:14 who say to God, *'Leave us alone! We have no desire to know your ways.'* How sad this is! And yet it is even sadder than we might think, because it applies to the church as it does to the world. The problem under discussion is not usually considered very deeply, let alone believed. Such unbelief clearly demonstrates itself in many ways. We rarely meet people who are not more or less satisfied with themselves and their lot in life. Many people in 'industrially developed' nations, if pressed, might say that life goes well for them and that they have few complaints. Other than some shortfall in the more materialistic and frivolous things, they have no particular wants or necessities. They would never understand why folk should be unsatisfied with the condition of their souls, or about the evil in their own heart or of their spiritual danger. They understand very little about these things. Most of the people we meet are quiet and at rest in their spirits, although they exist in 'the company of the dead.' (See Proverbs 21:16). They sleep in a sound and comforting skin, unaware of any danger. Thoughts of their actual condition never relieve them of even so much as one night's sleep. There are no challenges to their relationships with God; all is at peace with them because 'the strong man' keeps the house. (See Matthew 12:29.) It is a rare thing to find people, churchgoing or otherwise, who are devoted to the kingdom of God, and occupied with it in their thinking, either alone or in company, in writing or in teaching; or to find someone who has seriously thought about the matter. There are many concerned with 'church' and the things of 'church' and the spirituality of church from the convinced traditionalist to the joyous charismatic, but not many concerned with the kingdom.

It is even more rare to see any soul humbled in spirit and broken in heart because they are not sure of the way, or whose spirit seems to bleed under the weight of a heavy load. Nowhere can we hear anyone crying out, 'Friends, brothers and sisters, what shall we do to be saved?' (see Acts 16:30); or, 'How shall we come into the right way?' (see Isaiah 2:3). There seem to be few such questions troubling the public conscience, Christian or otherwise, and no wonder really —they seem to be in a 'deep sleep'. (See Proverbs 19:15.)

There would seem to be quite enough evidence here to prove our ignorance of the kingdom and lack of spiritual common sense, but it is the Holy Spirit who will *"convict the world of guilt with regard to sin and righteousness and judgment"* (John 16:8). We have to recognise and accept that, *It is not for man to direct his steps* (Jeremiah 10:23), that is to say that nothing he can do can or will ever provide a way for him to get to the kingdom. The statement that Jesus is the Way rules out all other ways and means. That we cannot do anything to help ourselves onto the road to the kingdom is made more obvious when we understand these things:

1. Our own way is evil by nature (see Proverbs 4:14).

2. We cannot turn around to see the kingdom, neither do we seem to want to. We have to be re-born first (see John 3:3).

3. We think that we are safe; no one can convince us otherwise. *There is a way that seems right to a man, but in the end it leads to death* (Proverbs 14:12).

4. Every one of us has our own favourite way which we turn to, some one thing or other or some way of conducting our religious or our spiritual life which we are satisfied with, that we think will be quite sufficient to carry us through, and there we go on, contentedly, like wandering sheep. *We all, like sheep, have gone astray, each of us has turned to his own way; and the* LORD *has laid on him the iniquity of us all*. (Isaiah 53:6).

5. Whichever way this way we are on turns out to be, even if it is a false way, we depend on it (see Hosea 10:13). We rely on it as the way to heaven's gate, little knowing that it will fail us in the end, and that along with our hope and self-confidence, it will perish at our death.

We cannot be surprised, then, to see men and women *going about so much*, as it says in Jeremiah 2:36, as if they could discover the way for themselves, or somehow fall on it by accident. What a deplorable sight, to see people weary from the teachings of so many 'friends' and 'false prophets' since childhood. *Each of them goes on in his error; there is not one that can save you*. (Isaiah 47:15).

So let us go on from here to look at some of those wrong and deceiving ways which some people stagger along to the point of weariness, all in vain. They choose to put their trust in ways and methods like these, but not one of them is safe and secure. They cannot all be covered here, so we shall discuss a basketful that are in the main popular and everyday:

1. Being good. Many of us deceive ourselves into doing good works, and into fine resolutions to do even greater good works, not necessarily out of compassion as the circumstances arise around us but from design or from peer pressure. We may suppose that this is all that is required of us. Unhappily for us, when we see the truth of it, all our plans and intentions are like the early morning cloud and fresh dew that soon burns up in the sunshine. Our plans and purposes rapidly run out of substance and flounder into

nothingness, quickly disappointing everyone involved. Perhaps they are made without sufficient planning, discussion or advice (see Proverbs 15:22) but they are attempted in our own strength. Many people then remain at this point, firmly resolving to do better at some time or other in the future. But our dreaming never comes to anything.

2. Some of us experience convictions and inner challenges, moving along a path which seems to lead from one to the other. Moments of clear understanding of our own behaviour patterns, or sometimes extracts from scripture, pierce us so deeply to the heart that we see ourselves as being in great error or greatly misguided or being subjected to divine correction. We feel we should cry out with Saul, *"I have sinned"* (1 Samuel 15:24). After this experience we do not go forward any further, those convictions either die out again or, at least, fail to work any further change in us. The mistake here is that we imagine, because we had some real conviction and sharp challenges through a powerful sermon or in a time of prayer or a reading of the scriptures, that all is going well with us, in what we suppose to be our state of sensitive spirituality. We forget that any Judas may have convictions which are much sharper than the ones we ever had —not forgetting Felix in Acts 24:25.

3. It must be said that sometimes those convictions are indeed followed by some sort of change. Some folk may deceive themselves dreadfully when this has happened, by coming to the conclusion that all is right with them, now that some great divine work has been done. They imagine that the way they now find themselves in is safe and sound, and must be the right one, because they have been convicted so effectively that many things have changed for them. This may well not be true at all. This may still be the way of darkness —it will not be the way of Christ if they have not come to him in true repentance about all these changes.

4. Many are satisfied with an image of outward civility and

spirituality. Such people could never be challenged over any 'big' sins, but that is all that can be said for them. They are wonderfully 'nice' people. But a wicked Pharisee could say exactly the same as they do, that one who could claim that he was not one of those *"robbers, evildoers, adulterers — or even like this tax collector"* (Luke 18:11). How many believers lead lives in almost complete ignorance of the kingdom of God and yet, with respect to their being 'nice', outstrip so many of us that profess to be Christians? (See Luke 18:21ff.)

5. Some may grow into much more than plain civility, reaching a kind of semblance of holiness, an outward performance of religious duties, like reading, leading prayer, preaching, and going on like this when this is their own way and not necessarily the right way. After all, the virgins still had their lamps and, when it got dark, they still waited for the groom. (See Matthew 25:1ff.) And surely great numbers of us will say, thinking we have found the right way to the kingdom, *'We ate and drank with you, and you taught in our streets.' But he will reply, 'I don't know you or where you come from. Away from me, all you evildoers!'* (See Luke 13:26f).

In our Bible reading we often see the Jews of the New Testament greatly absorbed in their religious duties, and the business of ensuring correct enactment, yet the Lord rejected them. (See Isaiah 1:11–15 and 66:3.)

6. Knowing a lot of things deceives a lot of people. We are apt to think that because we can talk authoritatively about matters of religion, have enough wisdom and intelligence to help other people in their difficult places, teach and preach extracts from scripture with great confidence, and the like, that therefore somehow we are doing well. Unhappily, this is the top of a slippery slope to stand on. The Pharisees sat in Moses' seat, much respected and teaching what to them would have been sound doctrine; and yet they were heart-enemies to Jesus. (See Matthew 23.) And perhaps

many of us will eventually find ourselves trying to plead our way into heaven by claiming that we have prophesied in his name. (See Matthew 7:22.) Knowledge can sometimes only serve to puff us up. (See 1 Corinthians 13:2.) But for many of us it is essential for the proper teaching and upbringing of the disciples around us. Some of us may from time to time successfully escape worldly pollution through the knowledge of the Lord and Saviour Jesus Christ, yet still become entangled in that knowledge and overcome by it. In this way our latter end is worse than the beginning. (See 2 Peter 2:20–22.) Knowledge, of course, is good, but it is not Christ, and so it is not the way to the Father and his kingdom.

7. Following on from the point just made, the growth of a kind of sober seriousness and determination in the performance of our duties, and in our seeking God, all of which we might be calling 'Christian maturity', deceives a number of us into believing that we have found the right way. Unaware of our own self-deception in taking what we do very seriously, we imagine that therefore all is well. Did Jesus not warn us that: *"Not everyone who says to me, 'Lord, Lord,' will enter the kingdom of heaven, but only he who does the will of my Father who is in heaven"* (Matthew 7:21)? Not everyone is on the right road to the kingdom because they persist in walking the way that they do with God (because they know of no other way and have matured in the way that they go about things). They cry over and over again for the Lord's blessing in developing their life's work and calling, yet progress is painfully slow, hard work that scarcely moves at all. The foolish virgins seemed serious and earnest enough, when they were determined to go on waiting through the night with the others. In the end they found themselves crying out, *"Sir, Sir.... Open the door for us"* (Matthew 25:11), but they were kept out of the wedding banquet.

Many of us turn away from understanding such verses, not wanting to think that we may have fallen prey to some secret form of hypocrisy. To many it is inconceivable that some will not get through. (See Matthew 7:13 and Luke 13:24).

8. It is easy to be deceived when we are looked on by other godly, discerning people and ministers, and are thought of by them to be good and serious Christians. If such folk themselves are held to be good and serious seekers after God, it becomes difficult to hold any opinion to the contrary. But the day is coming when many things will be discovered, and other people's approval will not count for anything, *For it is not the one who commends himself who is approved, but the one whom the Lord commends* (2 Corinthians 10:18). For this reason Timothy is encouraged by Paul: *Do your best to present yourself to God as one approved, a workman who does not need to be ashamed and who correctly handles the word of truth* (2 Timothy 2:15).

Men look only at the exterior and cannot see into the heart, but God searches the heart. It can be an easy thing to mislead other people, but God will not be deceived.

9. It is also easy to assume that we are on the right road if we have been generally accepted by the church and elevated into a place of leadership of some kind when, for all that advancement, the heart may be less than whole. The Pharisee in Luke 18:12 fasted twice a week and gave much to the poor, and was still not in line with the things of Christ.

10. On the other hand everything within may be a sunny meadow of peace and quiet, and it would be easy here to suppose that nothing is wrong. Nothing occurs that upsets the conscience. The heart does not accuse its owner of any falsehood or any manipulation of others. Such wanderers in sunny meadows do everything according to their own light. No doubt the young man in Luke 18:21 spoke according to his own judgement and his own light when he said, *"All these I have kept since I was a boy,"*

Paul says to the Sanhedrin about himself, in Acts 23:1, *"My brothers, I have fulfilled my duty to God in all good conscience to this day."* In saying this he meant that even while he was an unconverted Pharisee he had never gone against his conscience, but had always walked according to his own understanding of things, his own light. *"I too was convinced that I ought to do all that was possible to oppose the name of Jesus of Nazareth"* (Acts 26:9).

11. Their own enthusiasm for the faith might be deceiving quite a number of people into thinking that their way is authentic, simply because they are enthusiastic about the way they do everything concerning their role in church and about the kingdom. They imagine that this enthusiasm about God is pure. Paul, when still a Pharisee, was himself very enthusiastic and determined. Out of enthusiasm for the way he was following, he persecuted the church, *as for zeal, persecuting the church; as for legalistic righteousness, faultless* (Philippians 3:6). *Come with me and see my zeal for the Lord* (2 Kings 10:16). This attitude is well summed up in a discussion about the Jews in Romans 10:2f., *For I can testify about them that they are zealous for God, but their zeal is not based on knowledge. Since they did not know the righteousness that comes from God and sought to establish their own, they did not submit to God's righteousness.* Then again we can read that, *"They will put you out of the synagogue; in fact, a time is coming when anyone who kills you will think he is offering a service to God"* (John 16:2).

Some also claim that they are, beyond question, in the right way to finding the King and the kingdom, because they are far more strict than others in their beliefs and lifestyles. They will not even socialise with those who are not the same as they are. They say, *'Keep away; don't come near me, for I am too sacred for you!' Such people are smoke in my nostrils, a fire that keeps burning all day* (Isaiah 65:5). It would be terrible to be deceived in this area so it would not be a bad thing for the reader to test himself against this list while there is still a possibility of putting things right.

Again, remember that there is only one true and living way, and there is only the one way for all of us. There is only *one Mediator between God and men* (1 Timothy 2:5).

The most important and most obvious thing of all is that Jesus Christ is the way to the Father, the one and only way, the sovereign and excellent way, and he alone is the way. There is no other. *"Salvation is found in no one else, for there is no other name under heaven given to men by which we must be saved"* (Acts 4:12).

4

LOOKING FOR THE RIGHT GATEWAY

Now for those of us who would travel along this way to the Father and to the kingdom of Christ, we must have a clear picture of Jesus reigning at the heart of his kingdom. To seek first that kingdom is, therefore, to set out in the first place to find him. *"I am the gate; whoever enters through me will be saved"* (John 10:9).

A word of caution should be offered here, before setting out on the way to the kingdom. It is vital to find the right gateway. *"I tell you the truth, the man who does not enter the sheep pen by the gate, but climbs in by some other way, is a thief and a robber"* (John 10:1).

There are some attitudes of the heart which no one who takes the true gospel for themselves can avoid, proofs that the hearer has accepted the real Jesus Christ, crucified and risen, who is offered to us in that gospel. The acceptance of the different, false, unbiblical pictures of Christ mentioned earlier does not produce these proofs, and the fact of their absence from our spiritual walk might be an indicator of which 'lord' is being worshipped.

There must be a deep acceptance (conviction) of our innate ability to sin. This is the state of being 'biased towards sin' mentioned in an earlier chapter, giving us a natural inclination to fall away from God's presence. Our natural soul tends towards living in a state of absence from him, *for all have sinned and fall short of the glory of God* (Romans 3:23).

We have come under God's death sentence as a result of one

man's offences. (See Romans 5:15.) We have been made into natural-born sinners by that one individual man's disobedience (see verse 19), and therefore put under death's reigning power (see verse 17), and subject to the condemnation that came onto all of us, (see verse 18). So we are what might be considered 'normal' and 'average' for modern mankind. Like other generations, we suffer from that original hereditary bias towards sin, the symptom of which is a heart that, left to its own devices and devoid of God's Spirit, fills with dislike for God, becomes averse to him and his ways, and takes a stand in open opposition to him and to his holy laws and his working. This is mankind's natural state. Those of us who have not yet come free of that original enmity towards the name of Jesus, even some practising churchmen, tend to contradict and resist him. We give our position away by despising and undervaluing his love gifts, stubbornly refusing his goodness and continuous offers of miraculous mercy, and persisting in rebellion and heart-opposition. We not only reject his miraculous acts of kindness and offers of mercy, but condemn them, or have grave doubts about them, cynically trampling them under foot and spreading doubt among the congregation of the Lord, as if we somehow feel embittered towards him.

This conviction, not so much of mankind's general and frightening state but of the dreadful condition of the individual, is usually not something which is worked out in the mind by our intellect or theology. It may begin with a word carried home to the heart by the finger of God, fear of approaching death, maybe a serious illness, or a set of intolerable life circumstances. It is a real thing, a heart-reaching conviction, that we are naturally evil. It seems peculiar to the individual, quite clear in its interpretation, touching the heart with fear of God and fear for the person's own eventual future. It causes us to cry out anxiously, "What shall I do to be saved?" It will then make the soul willing to listen to, and long to study, what hopes and promises of grace and mercy there are in the gospel, and to take a firm hold of the way of salvation which can be found there.

There must be present a measure of humility. Under the conviction of our bias towards sin, we are bowed and quietened in the presence of God. It is not so easy now to speak of our own achievements or about the self-satisfaction we may have in pleasurable living. Most noticeably, we cease altogether from thinking about our own 'righteous acts' because we can now see them all as 'filthy rags'. (See Isaiah 64:6).

But whatever was to my profit I now consider loss for the sake of Christ. What is more, I consider everything a loss compared to the surpassing greatness of knowing Christ Jesus my Lord, for whose sake I have lost all things. I consider them rubbish, that I may gain Christ (Philippians 3:7f).

The unbeliever's naturally self-confident and disdainful attitude towards Christ and his followers will be cast down by this same conviction. When we grasp its truth, we will now no longer have any conceited thoughts about ourselves, or of anything we ever did or can do. The Lord resists the proud, but gives grace to the humble. (See James 4:6; 1 Peter 5:5). *I live in a high and holy place, but also with him who is contrite and lowly in spirit, to revive the spirit of the lowly and to revive the heart of the contrite* (Isaiah 57:15). The one who humbles himself like a little child will be seen as the greatest in the kingdom of heaven. (See Matthew 18:4, and 23:12; Luke 14:11, and 18:14).

There should be a sense of despair at ever getting out of this disastrous situation by ourselves, or by anything or through any help we can organise through other people. The closer the seeker comes to the kingdom, the more he loses all expectation of any eventual 'leg up' into heaven from any good nature that he may suppose he has: works of charity, good intentions, good deeds, other people's commendation, many prayers, a regular churchgoing life, a sober and harmless walking through life, or anything else inside or outside him which is not Christ. We can fool ourselves that such good attributes only occur because Christ is in us, but the simple fact remains: they are not Christ. As long as we have the smallest hope of getting into heaven without Christ, we will not come to him.

The necessary change of heart may not be as easy as it sounds. Mankind's natural way of thinking hankers after the old ideas of the way of salvation through works or behaviour, so much so that we find it difficult to accept any other route.

It is important, then, that before we can wholeheartedly come to Jesus Christ in his kingdom, and accept him for who and what he is and for what he has done, we separate ourselves from the lies we have been thinking about, and recognise that — of all our prayers, fasting, times of weeping before him, duties to the community fulfilled, reformations in our own souls, sufferings, good wishes and good deeds towards other people — none of these things are keys that can give access to the kingdom of God on earth, or to heaven after this life. There must be a deliberate and continuous, rational and determined, letting go of all the things in ourselves on which our heart is often easily set which are opposed to God. In being convinced of the vanity of all things through which we might have been hoping for a good life, we must now set out to loose their grip on us, turning our backs on the power that pulls us towards them, away from the centre of the kingdom. We must learn to say to them, *'Away with you!'* (Isaiah 30:22). This is what it means to deny ourselves, something we must do before we become disciples of Jesus. (See Matthew 16:24.) This is to forget our people and our father's house (see Psalm 45:10) and figuratively to pluck out our right eye and to cut off our right arm (see Matthew 5:29f).

There should be a growing understanding of the nature of the gospel, of the new covenant, and of the way in which God chose to glorify himself as he releases his grace in the salvation of his people. We should be showing signs of going deeper and deeper into the river of grace that runs through the kingdom. (See Ezekiel 47f and Revelation 22:1f.) God the Father sent Jesus Christ his Son to us, of his free grace (gift) and mercy. This is how we understand the ministry of the one who is now King of the kingdom we seek. God became man; the nature of Jesus Christ, therefore, is both divine and human. He fulfilled the law, and died the cursed death of the cross, to satisfy justice and pay the ransom for our redemption. In all this work, our Lord was both a servant (see Isaiah 42:1; 49:6; 52:13, and 53:11; also Zechariah 3:8 and Matthew 12:18) and he was Master to those who have become his disciples. He came fully equipped for everything he would be undertaking. (See Isaiah 42:1; 61:1,2 and Matthew 12:18.)

The ministry the Son would carry out accorded perfectly with the will of the Father. It was God's plan of redemption. Thus the prophecy was fulfilled that the Lord laid on him, or caused to meet together on him, 'the iniquity of us all'. (See Isaiah 53:6). So, in due time,

Surely he took up our infirmities
and carried our sorrows,
yet we considered him stricken by God,
smitten by him, and afflicted.
But he was pierced for our transgressions,
he was crushed for our iniquities;
the punishment that brought us peace was upon him,
and by his wounds we are healed.

Isaiah 53:4f.

Yet it was the LORD's will to crush him
and cause him to suffer,
and though the LORD makes his life a guilt offering,
he will see his offspring and prolong his days,

and the will of the LORD will prosper in his hand.
After the suffering of his soul,
he will see the light of life and be satisfied;
by his knowledge my righteous servant will justify many,
and he will bear their iniquities.
Therefore I will give him a portion among the great,
and he will divide the spoils with the strong,
because he poured out his life unto death,
and was numbered with the transgressors.
For he bore the sin of many,
and made intercession for the transgressors.

Isaiah 53:10–12

What the law was powerless to do because it was weakened by our sinful nature, God did himself by sending his own Son in the likeness of sinful man to be a sin offering. And so he condemned sin in sinful man.

Romans 8:3

...in order that the righteous requirements of the law might be fully met in us," (verse 4). In this way "God made him who had no sin to be sin for us, so that in him we might become the righteousness of God.

2 Corinthians 5:21

...so Christ was sacrificed once to take away the sins of many people; and he will appear a second time, not to bear any more sin, but to bring salvation to those who are waiting for him.

Hebrews 9:28

He himself bore our sins in his body on the tree, so that we might die to sins and live for righteousness....

1 Peter 2:24

There surely has to be some growing understanding of the great mystery of the gospel, where we can find declared *the manifold wisdom of God* (Ephesians 3:10), and the amazing planning of God in sending his Son to die as prescribed by the law, so that we condemned sinners can live, and go to the bosom of God, redeemed, *not with perishable things such as silver or gold that you were redeemed from the empty way of life handed down to you from your forefathers, but with the precious blood of Christ, a lamb without blemish or defect* (1 Peter 1:18f).

A vital part of man's conviction of natural bias towards sin must be a belief in the total adequacy and abundant sufficiency of the way of salvation through this crucified Christ. Without this sense of certainty and total effectiveness the soul will not be pressured to leave all its previously preferred directions. We must be absolutely sure, not only that this is the only way to salvation but that salvation will certainly come if we follow Jesus who is the way.

There must be a satisfaction with the gospel, acceptance that the old self is to be crucified with Christ. We have no way of finding the kingdom of God without our heart being open to Jesus Christ as Lord and Saviour, and receiving him. The soul must embrace and receive him. (See John 1:12.) The convicted and converted sinner must have Jesus as his Lord, Master, Saviour, King, priest and prophet. He must surrender himself to Jesus as his leader and commander, firmly resolving to follow him in all the things he has taught us. What has been described as the great exchange takes place. Until we utterly surrender, repenting and believing in Jesus, we are living in our sins, not living in Christ; and there is no inheriting the fruits of his redemption, no justification before God, and no pardon in this life or at the last judgement if we continue living in our sins. Having repented, believed, and surrendered our lives to Jesus Christ, receiving him personally as our only Lord and our only Saviour we are to go on believing, abiding in him, and overcoming the attacks of the enemy.

The soul should be developing an attitude of leaning towards him, resting on him and on the fact of his perfect sacrifice. The satisfied soul of the kingdom citizen sits down here, in the cool shade of the Saviour's sure and certain guarantees. We are to believe on him, to rest on him. (See John 3:18; 1 Peter 2:6.) In scripture, salvation has past, present and future meanings. Of one who has been born again, it can be said with scriptural accuracy, that he has been saved by grace through faith in Jesus — the sacrifice of Jesus on the cross from the *penalty* of sin — and he is *being saved* through the sanctifying work of the Holy Spirit from the power of sin; and he looks forward to being saved (in the world to come) from the *presence* of sin.

'Resting' in Jesus Christ is the result in this life of being able to cast onto him the punishing weight of a broken covenant, of the well-deserved anger of God, of a guilty conscience and the effects on the individual of the curse of the broken law. This is, in part, what it means to *put on* the Lord Jesus, (see Romans 13:14); to cover ourselves with his righteousness which protects us in the face of justice, to stand safely dressed in this armour of God against the accusations of sin. This is what it means to run in through his gates and behind his walls as our city of refuge, making us safe from the thief of abundant life. This is how it feels to be safe from the storm of God's righteous anger against sin, and to sit in the shade from the heat of his rage (see Isaiah 25:4), like a shelter from the wind and a refuge from the storm, *like streams of water in the desert and the shadow of a great rock in a thirsty land* (Isaiah 32:2).

It is his will that we should die to ourselves and follow him into the kingdom —that he should be our only reason for being there. In the very moment that Christ is seen as the way, the only way, and it is realised that there is no other possible way, and that living without him is to be lost for ever, then we climb through the smallest of gates and onto the narrowest of roads that leads to heaven, the way being narrow only because we need to walk on a path that is no wider than the width of his footprints.

The kingdom seeker will not necessarily always be able to discern easily whether another is walking in the right way, though of course there are certain biblical hallmarks that distinguish every believer. We should understand that some of the outward effects of surrendering our lives to Jesus, finding the right road to the kingdom, are not the same or as immediately evident in all of us. For some of us it may be more lively, demonstrative and active, like the centurion's faith, that led him to argue with great logic. (See Matthew 8:8f.) He was one in whom Jesus found great faith, greater than he had found elsewhere. A person's faith may look like that of the woman of Canaan in Matthew 15:21. In others, the outward expression of what is in the heart may appear weaker. For some, it is much more difficult to express our faith and feelings clearly. Sometimes it is mixed with much fear (see Matthew 8:26), and sometimes with such humility that it fully recognises its own great weakness (see Mark 9:24).

In some of us, the acts and acting out of this living in the kingdom may be clearly and easily discernible to ourselves and by others. In others it may be covered over by so thick a layer of doubt, unbelief, pride, jealousy or other corruption that the evidence of living in the kingdom is hardly seen at all. For some, the evidence for this living in the kingdom and the corresponding faith in its King may have strong and easily perceptible outworking, as the kingdom seeker wrestles through waves of discouragement and opposition, as did the woman of Canaan. Such a kingdom seeker is run through with determined resolve, saying with Job, *'Though he slay me, yet will I hope in him; I will surely defend my ways to his face'* (Job 13:15), and the forceful taking of the kingdom (see Matthew 11:12) can certainly involve firm determination. In others the desire for kingdom living may be so weak that the least opposition and discouragement may be quite sufficient to make the soul give up hope, trampled by despair about ever overcoming and winning through. Such souls may become bruised reeds. For some of us, the longing to live in the kingdom may be firmly entrenched, and we are quietly determined to stay with it (see Isaiah 26:3f), trusting in him. (See Psalm 125:1.) However, a weak faith today may become stronger within a short time. Christ, who laid the foundation, can and will finish the building, for all his works are perfect.

This finding of the right way to the kingdom is a business of enormous importance, and yet many of us are not very troubled or exercised about it. We deceive ourselves with foolish ways of thinking. We think we have been kingdom people all along; we never doubted God's grace and goodwill. We always had a good heart for God, although we never knew what originally awakened our conscience, or had any real sense of the wrath of God and the protection of Calvary. Or we may suppose, because God is merciful, that he will not be severe or even insistent upon anything changing in us. We forget that he is a just God and a God of truth, and he will do as he has said. Or we imagine that we can delegate responsibility for our own faith to our church leaders. Or we decide that we will make a commitment later to slip through the gate at a more convenient time, and fail to see the cunning sleight of Satan's hand in this attitude. 'Very soon' can be too late. All these imaginings lead us into believing that the gate and the way to the kingdom are broad and easy to travel when, in reality, the opposite is true.

5

THE SANCTIFYING ROAD

Having passed into the kingdom through the gateway called justification, the kingdom seeker is now called to set off along the way, Jesus Christ, who is the sanctifying road. The new life given to us at our new birth has begun. If we sit down now we will have nowhere to go in this life other than the normal routine of ups and downs, of secular successes and failings.

The sanctifying walk of the kingdom seeker carries us deeper and deeper into the kingdom of God, always looking up ahead to the end of the road where there is another set of gates, this time wide open, behind which lie the mansions already prepared for us. The soul's interior journey from the badlands of the nomadic life into the enjoyed presence of God is beautiful. Once justified, kingdom seekers need no longer fearfully hesitate at the entrance to the Holy of Holies. God wills that we should push on into his presence and live our whole life there.

But kingdom walking should not be conceived as a kind of self-improvement. True goodness forgets itself and goes out to do the right thing for no other reason than that it is right —because it is the will of our Lord and Saviour. And yet the effect on us if we take full advantage of the walk is that we grow in grace. This growing in grace was never meant to be optional, it is a duty.

You ought to live holy and godly lives . . . . So then, dear friends, since you are looking forward to this, make every effort to be found spotless, blameless and at peace with him (2 Peter 3:11, 14).

This growing in grace along the way of sanctification is variously referred to in scripture: *"If a man remains in me and I in him, he will bear much fruit"* (John 15:5), so, *add to your faith goodness* (2 Peter 1:5–7). In this way, *we will in all things grow up into him who is the Head, that is, Christ* (Ephesians 4:15). And we should work out our salvation with fear and trembling. (See Philippians 2:12), perfecting holiness out of reverence for God. (2 Corinthians 7:1), so that, *we too may live a new life* (Romans 6:4). We cannot wander off the path again, *but rather offer yourselves to God, as those who have been brought from death to life* (Romans 6:13); *in order that we might bear fruit to God* (Romans 7:4); *so that we serve in the new way of the Spirit* (Romans 7:6). Some of these verses express the nature of this change, some show the root and some the fruit of it, but all of them display a special work to us, that is becoming holy, gracious, and growing in grace.

This, then, is a special daily work in every kingdom seeker. Without Jesus Christ we cannot see this work started, still less make any progress in it. We would not have found the right gate and we could not walk along the right road. So the real question now is: How are we to take advantage of the gifts and grace of Christ for this work of sanctification?

There are a few useful pointers here.

1. The kingdom seeker might like to consider what an attractive idea this would be to self as well as to others: to be wearing this new man, created in the image of God. (See Ephesians 4:23.) The seeker would have a growing joy in God, giving thanks to the Father, *who has qualified you to share in the inheritance of the saints in the kingdom of light* (Colossians 1:12), *that you may live a life worthy of the Lord and may please him in every way: bearing fruit in every good work, growing in the knowledge of God* (Colossians 1:10). *He will be an instrument for noble purposes, made holy, useful to the Master and prepared to do any good work* (2 Timothy 2:21).

2. Although we cannot carry out this business of sanctification in ourselves, we should always remember that it is our duty to be available and open to this work, and we are all called by God to submit to it joyfully. At our conversion, the farmer sows the seed of grace in our souls, new habits are infused, a new life is given to us, and the heart of stone is changed into a heart of flesh. These things cannot even be brought into being in the first place by anything that a kingdom seeker can do apart from the sovereign grace of God, who initiates and sustains what happens. The work of ongoing sanctification and growth in grace must be effected by the Spirit of Jesus now dwelling and working within. That is why it is called the sanctification of the Spirit. (See 2 Thessalonians 2:13; 1 Peter 1:2; also Romans 15:16; 1 Corinthians 6:11.) It can still often be found that there is little or no growing in grace after the seeker has come through the gate and set out on the way. It is as though he has taken only a few steps and then stopped. One possible reason for failure to grow in grace, or to progress in this kingdom work, is that the seeker has not originally come through the right gate but through some kind of replica or counterfeit of it. This might mean an insufficient conversion, or perhaps no conversion at all. Another cause is the seeker's not acting as if he really believes in this. We sometimes set about the work as if we ourselves could master it and do without any divine help. It is not we who do the work, but it is our duty to remain open always to its being done in us. It is vital that the kingdom seeker should abide, live, and go about life's business, trusting completely in this truth, or he will be throttling the process of ongoing sanctification.

3. Kingdom seekers, in setting out along the way, should not trust to their own strength, to any long held habits of grace, to former skills, training and experiences or to their wisdom and knowledge of life. This is not to suggest that any of these things should be totally ignored or thrown away as they might be used by God as he goes about the business of imparting his sanctification and

grace. It would not be right, though, to attempt to prescribe to him how he is to use us.

4. The seeker who longs to grow in grace should remember that Christ is proposed to us as an example to imitate. As we walk deeper into the kingdom, we should set Christ continually in front of us as our pattern, so that we can follow his steps. (See 1 Peter 1:15; 2:21.)

5. The kingdom seeker should adopt a frame of thinking that holds Christ as the root stock into which the branches are grafted. He should adopt a permanent desire to suck sap, life and strength from him so that he can walk, work and grow as a Christian should. The kingdom seeker will then grow up in him, being a branch of him, and will produce fruit in him. Christ himself tells us that the branches cannot produce this fruit unless the disciple abides in the vine. (See John 15.) It follows that, as it is trust in Jesus Christ that keeps the branch attached to the vine, so it is by the same trust in Christ that the branches will produce fruit. This trust is the way we cling onto Christ as the vine providing us with sap, life and strength. Jesus, of course, has easily enough sap to support all the branches, for the fullness of the Godhead dwells in him. Life, strength and all the necessary equipping for ministry flows from Christ into those kingdom seekers who are believing, trusting and obeying him.

6. To keep this sap flowing, kingdom seekers must stay open to scripture, guard against grieving the Holy Spirit and be open to him constantly. Questioning Christ's faithfulness or disbelieving it will put obstacles in the way. One common error is to pray for healing as if it might not happen. God is constant and unchangeable love, so it grieves the Spirit that we should think or speak of him in any other way.

So the kingdom seeker stays open by looking and waiting, drawing from him, seeking what we need from him, and guarding against anything and everything that might grieve his Spirit.

Here, then, is a picture of an earnest, serious and hungry kingdom seeker, looking to Jesus, on a holy, sober, humble and watchful walk. This is what it means to open wide the mouth so that he can fill it; to lie down on one's face before him, so that the beams of light that emanate from him can beat down on us, warm us and revive us; and to be a beggar at the King's gate, waiting day and night on him until he dispenses the alms.

7. The seeker must lay hold firmly of Christ's death on the cross, and his resurrection. His saving death on the cross bought access for us into the kingdom and all its gifts and benefits. His crucifixion removed the padlock and chain from the gate of justification. What flows from this is vital for carrying on the work of grace and sanctification in the soul of the kingdom seeker. God has *blessed us in the heavenly realms with every spiritual blessing in Christ* (Ephesians 1:3). The kingdom seeker needs to be aware that the blessing of our forgiveness and new life have been purchased at an enormous cost: the blood of Jesus Christ. *His divine power has given us everything we need for life and godliness through our knowledge of him who called us by his own glory and goodness* (2 Peter 1:3). This way of thinking of the grace that came to us through the cross should encourage the soul into a constant state of expectant waiting; we are to look for the flow of spiritual blessings in showers of grace which will cause us to flourish and grow more fruit.

8. Anchoring our understanding of the kingdom in the death of Christ, kingdom seekers are mindful, too, of his resurrection, and the fact that we are raised in and with him; his resurrection is a certain guarantee of our sanctification.

The apostle wrote (in Romans 6:4,5,11,13) by way of encouragement to us that, *We were therefore buried with him through baptism into death in order that, just as Christ was raised from the dead through the glory of the Father, we too may live a new life. If we have been united with him like this in his death,*

we will certainly also be united with him in his resurrection . . . .
In the same way, count yourselves dead to sin but alive to God in
Christ Jesus . . . . Do not offer the parts of your body to sin, as
instruments of wickedness, but rather offer yourselves to God, as
those who have been brought from death to life . . . .

9. The resurrection of Christ then brings us another area for optimism and confidence in this work of sanctification. Scripture makes mention of the power of his resurrection, in Philippians 3:10. Through the very fact of his resurrection, we can draw goodness and strength from Christ by faith, because we are members of the body of which he is the risen, living head. It is because of Christ's resurrection that we can live to God's glory and manifest fruit that glorifies him, and we can do this in newness of life because of the work of the Spirit. (See Romans 7:4,6.)

10. We can also rest assured that the business of our sanctification will continue, if we are open to it, because Christ is permanently interceding for us. We remember the prayer of Jesus: *"Sanctify them by the truth; your word is truth"* (John 17:17), and we know that he was always heard by the Father. (See John 11:41f.)

The kingdom seeker should now be seeing Christ as communicating with the Father to start and finish this work of sanctification. We also know that his death on the cross provided all the promised and necessary freedoms from the 'old man' of sin. At the same time, Jesus carries out and confirms our ongoing sanctification; he guarantees the work. Because of all these things, it should be easy to trust him to actually confer on us the requisite graces, so we can cast the burden of the work onto him, trusting him completely. We know absolutely that he will do this because of his relationship with us, his people. He will work his works through us, bear all our burdens, perfect his work of sanctification begun in us, present us to himself as a holy bride, ensure that *the Spirit of God lives in you* (Romans 8:9) and, *give life to your mortal bodies through his Spirit* (verse 11), *because those who are led by the Spirit of God are sons of God* (verse 14). On the one hand, the kingdom seeker is to commit the work of sanctification to Christ, leaving all the stress of such business to him. On the other hand, the kingdom seeker must never think he needs to do nothing about it. By whatever methods and means are at his disposal, he is to recognise and roll over the burden of this work to Christ, but remain sensitively aware of every prompting of the Holy Spirit.

CAUTIONS
Here are a few words of care and caution for the reader, in the hope of preventing mistakes.

1. Beware of thinking that perfection can be got here: the perfect measure of the stature of the fullness of Christ is on its way, but until then the body will be perfecting and edifying, through the work of the ministry. (See Ephesians 4:12f.) Kingdom seekers must never think of sitting down and resting on any measure of grace which they might have reached; they must be growing in grace, going from strength to strength. *Forgetting what is behind and straining toward what is ahead, I press on toward the goal to win the prize for which God has called me heavenward in Christ Jesus* (Philippians 3:13f). Let us all live in the constant conviction of our shortcomings, and so work out our salvation with fear and trembling.

2. It would be good to remember that there may be some progress made in the way of holiness which the kingdom seeker does not necessarily recognise. This may be because the size of the growth is small enough to be scarcely discernible, or perhaps because even where the growth in itself can be noticed, the Lord might think it good, for his own reasons, to hide it from us.

There are many things that may happen in the course of sanctification, but the proof of ongoing sanctification is never the particular vocation —whether solitary contemplation, full energetic work with the poor, or any other particular calling. What really matters, whatever walk of life we may engage in, is that there should be an ever increasing zeal to see the kingdom of God displayed in our lives.

3. There may be a great growing in holiness, which might not necessarily be in the most obvious area that the kingdom seeker was hoping for. When he thinks he is not growing in love towards God, he may be growing in humility (which is also part of the 'new man' of grace). It may be that he cannot discern any longed-for growth of ministry or growth of knowledge, but there may be, for example, a growth in affection and tenderness.

4. We should be careful not to think that there is no growth in grace because it has not come in the way we expected. It may be that some kingdom seekers are fond of some particular ministry techniques and fashions and it is easy to imagine that, if ever we can become good people, it would be by the continuous application of those methods. God may check us in our lack of wisdom by taking us another way.

5. The act of pursuing sanctification, 'panting' after it with singleness of heart, is no small measure of holiness. Nehemiah did not think this was a small thing, when he said, *"O LORD, let your ear be attentive to the prayer of this your servant and to the prayer of your servants who delight in revering your name"* (Nehemiah 1:11).

6. Whatever measure of sanctification the kingdom seeker reaches in life, he must take special care never to think of this as being in any way responsible for his having been accepted and justified —that was a free gift, received through faith in Jesus Christ, by grace alone.

6

THE WOUNDS OF LIFE, THE WOUNDS OF DEATH

We have seen the humble and childlike kingdom seeker, having found the right gateway, then setting out through it and along the way to the centre of the kingdom. In passing through the gate of justification the goodness of Jesus Christ is his cloak of righteousness in the face of holy justice. *It is because of him that you are in Christ Jesus, who has become for us wisdom from God —that is, our righteousness, holiness and redemption* (1 Corinthians 1:30).

Having come through the right gate and become justified before God, the kingdom seeker can now make even further use of the riches of Christ and his kingdom for sanctification, this being an area in which kingdom seekers are often thoroughly exercised and perplexed.

Before we launch into this matter in detail, it should be remembered that the person taken with the idea of personal sanctification, received on the way that leads deeper into the kingdom, has to be someone who has already come through the valid and narrow gateway for righteousness and justification. Those who are strangers to Christ may well not yet have come through the gate and so might not yet have any access to Christ for our sanctification. One must be a kingdom seeker who has come through the right gateway before we can make use of the solid ground of sanctification laid down and waiting for us. We must first be *in him* before we can grow up in him and bring forth fruit in him. The first thing that we kingdom seekers have to attend to, therefore, is the state of our communion with Christ, and being clothed with his righteousness by faith. Then we have a right to all his benefits that are to be found in the kingdom.

But can a kingdom seeker approach Christ with confidence and yet still have doubts and misunderstandings about his state of regeneration? The answer lies in the bottomless grace of God. If the seeker has a deep desire to be made holy, and to grow more into the image of God to glorify him, all is well. If the seeker is full of zeal in searching for the kingdom, all is well. If he pants after personal holiness at least as much as he pursues life itself, then all is well. If he makes the search — first for justification and then for sanctification — his life's work, allowing his own shortcomings to sadden him a little every day, longing for the day when he is delivered from a body of death and has the old man wholly crucified, then all is well. Such a seeker does not need to question the depth or level of excitement of his conversion to Christ, as such an attitude as this 'spiritual panting' is unlikely to be found in anyone but a believer. Some seek to establish their own righteousness, and to be justified by their own works and inherent goodness. They may wish that they might be more holy and less guilty; they might long to find a way to be free of the power of some lust or other bad behaviour pattern which they find troublesome and destructive, yet they would retain and desire some other cherished lusts. In this way they keep hold of a heart still clinging to some offensive thing or other. But the gracious and humble kingdom seeker, with a growing respect for all God's commands, has not the slightest intention of trying to be justified before God by his works; neither does he study ecclesiastically 'correct' levels of penance and sanctification to achieve justification. His justification was given as he walked into the kingdom through the right gate; his sanctification comes along the way ahead.

So how is it that Christ himself becomes our sanctification?

THE WOUNDS OF LIFE, THE WOUNDS OF DEATH

We saw that, in 1 Corinthians 1:30, Paul declares that *Christ Jesus has become . . . our holiness*. Now, having come in through the gate, how should the kingdom seeker conduct himself along the way so that he can grow in grace, and perfect holiness in the fear of God? The kingdom seeker should understand that this sanctification is never brought about by his own hand. It is the work of God —Father, Son and Holy Spirit. The Father is said to prune the branches so that they can produce more fruit. (See John 15:1,2). The Son is also referred to as the one who has made atonement for the sins of his people. (See Hebrews 2:17). *Christ loved the church and gave himself up for her to make her holy, cleansing her by the washing with water through the word* (Ephesians 5:25f). It is also said that the Holy Spirit may sanctify us (see 2 Thessalonians 2:13, 1 Peter 1:2 and Romans 15:16). The Spirit expresses redeeming love, and the Spirit is truth, and the Spirit is the Holy Spirit. The fact that one of the first recorded actions of the Holy Spirit in the Gospels is an expression of redeeming love (see Matthew 1:18) makes us suspect that we should be emphasising his action in the sanctification of our souls. It is important that we think of him as the Spirit of holiness as well as the Spirit who labours in us for the salvation of the whole of mankind.

The process we are describing is therefore, demonstrably, thoroughly trinitarian. But our particular study here could be summarised by asking how it can be that we are said to be *sanctified in Christ Jesus* (1 Corinthians 1:2). Christ has ensured this work of cleaning his church by his work on the cross. He *suffered outside the city gate to make the people holy through his own blood* (Hebrews 13:12). He *gave himself for us to redeem us from all wickedness and to purify for himself a people that are his very own, eager to do what is good* (Titus 2:14). Our sanctification is the fruit of his death, for we are bought by his blood. He gave his life on the cross for his church, so that he could sanctify it. (See

Ephesians 5:25f). Once through the gate, kingdom seekers are considered to be already dead to sin in him. This is why the apostle tells us, in Romans 6:3–6, *Don't you know that all of us who were baptized into Christ Jesus were baptized into his death? We were therefore buried with him through baptism into death in order that, just as Christ was raised from the dead through the glory of the Father, we too may live a new life. If we have been united with him like this in his death, we will certainly also be united with him in his resurrection.* In this way the kingdom seeker who has gone through the gate has been united with Christ who was crucified, so evil can no longer have any dominion over him. This is a great comfort to kingdom seekers. Christ died a public and humiliating death, and each seeker becomes more and more united with that death. This process grows deeper as the sanctification grows deeper, as the seeker approaches the epicentre of the kingdom —Calvary. Because Christ is resurrected, the believer can now lead a rich resurrection life in the kingdom, with all that entails.

It follows, then, that *our old self was crucified with him so that the body of sin might be done away with, that we should no longer be slaves to sin —because anyone who has died has been freed from sin* (Romans 6:6f). The old tyrant who drags down the people of God received his death wounds at Christ's crucifixion, and need never be allowed to recover his former energy and activity levels, oppressing the people of God as he used to.

Jesus' resurrection from death is heaven's guarantee to us of sanctification. We have been buried with him by baptism, and just as he was raised from the dead we should also walk in newness of life. (See Romans 6:4.) In all this, kingdom seekers are said to be buried together with him, (verse 5), and we will live with him (verse 8), and so we are to think of ourselves as being alive in God, through Jesus Christ our Lord (verse 11). *And God raised us up with Christ and seated us with him in the heavenly realms in Christ Jesus* (Ephesians 2:6).

THE WOUNDS OF LIFE, THE WOUNDS OF DEATH

So what will happen to the humble seeker, having gone through the narrow gate and begun to spend the rest of life walking deeper into the kingdom? He becomes more sanctified, the process of growing in holiness. As we go on believing and go on repenting, God will cleanse us from all the sin we have committed, and will forgive all our sins of rebellion against him. (See Jeremiah 33:8; Ezekiel 37:23.) Now all the promises of the new covenant are confirmed to us in our Mediator, *For no matter how many promises God has made, they are "Yes" in Christ. And so through him the "Amen" is spoken by us to the glory of God* (2 Corinthians 1:20). Increasingly, God's power gives us everything that applies to life and godliness, through our growing knowledge of Christ who has called us towards his glory and virtue. (See 2 Peter 1:3f.) Through him we are given great and precious promises beyond all our expectations, so that we might be made partakers of the divine nature. Jesus prayed, *"Sanctify them by the truth; your word is truth"* (John 17:17). The Lord is praying that his disciples might be more and more sanctified. As that happened, they would be better fitted and qualified for the work of the ministry in which they were to be employed. What he prayed for them was not for them alone, but for all of us who are on the way through the kingdom. Kingdom working requires equipping, and Jesus' prayer enables that to happen.

Of course, the kingdom seeker remains fallible, and the path to holiness is not a smooth one. But, when we dirty ourselves again with new failings and acts of disobedience, a fountain has been provided for us to wash in. *On that day a fountain will be opened to the house of David and the inhabitants of Jerusalem, to cleanse them from sin and impurity* (Zechariah 13:1) —this fountain is Jesus' blood, which cleanses us from all sin. (See Hebrews 9:14, 1 John 1:7 and Revelation 1:5.)

We might remember, for our own encouragement, and our confidence in the purpose and effects of this work of sanctification, that there is a great deal of satisfaction that comes from doing kingdom work. The Lord's pleasure can only be imagined, as he watches the seed of his own ministry, and the fruits of his work on the cross, growing in the palm of his hand.

Now we must consider how the kingdom seeker should conduct himself along the way so that he can grow in grace. There are a few things to be careful about:

1. We should beware of the arrows of heartless gloom that may be directed at us, and be on our guard against giving way in the face of any discouragement. We must learn to ignore the language of unbelief and listening to Satan's suggestions on the apparent 'impossibility' of pressing on with the work of sanctification. Satan, and a deceitful heart, can soon muster up many hurdles, alleging that there are many insuperable difficulties in the way. As kingdom seekers we should keep up our heads in hope, and beware of agreeing with, and consequently multiplying, discouragements thrown at ourselves; nor must we even consider giving up. If we give up, then we would have neither heart nor hand for kingdom work, but would sit down and wring our hands in despair, as if overcome with discouragement and despondency.

2. We will have to beware of wilfully rejecting kingdom mercies, and of forgoing making use of the hope and *miraculous* strength of God in progressing sanctification in our mind and body, which Christ has made available to us, and of which he allows us to make full use. There is such an evil among God's children displayed when we fight against, or flee away from, those gifts and mercies that Christ has provided for us, out of his great love. Some of us simply do not dare to make use of these healing mercies with any degree of confidence, judging ourselves to be unworthy even though God has already decided that we are more than valuable.

3. We should beware of laying too much emphasis on the liturgies, sacraments, methods and means of healing and sanctification *in themselves*. It is true that the Lord has often thought fit to work

in and through various methods and means, but it is he himself who does the inward work.

4. Given that the means themselves cannot do anything unless he breathes on the situation, we should still be very careful of any careless way of performing the means without that certain seriousness and devotion that is required. *A curse on him who is lax in doing the Lord's work!* (Jeremiah 48:10). Here the special art of Christian churchmanship might be practised: we must be as devoted and serious in the use of whatever might be the accepted technique as if it really will affect the outcome of the proceedings. At the same time we have to be far removed from the methods and means, in our hopes and expectation. We need to be leaning on the Lord alone, and utterly depending on him for the blessing, as if we were not using any methods and means at all.

5. We should also guard against the quenching of the Spirit (see 1 Thessalonians 5:12); or the possibility of grieving the Spirit (see Ephesians 4:30) because of any unchristian and unsuitable way of going about things. This will greatly injure the process of our sanctification. It is by the Holy Spirit that the work of sanctification is carried on in the believer, and when the Spirit is disturbed, or stopped from working, how can we expect the work to go on?

6. We should beware of simply letting our sins drift into our history without repentance (see Psalm 51:10), and of committing any sin, especially those sins which David referred to as 'wilful' sins. (See Psalm 19:13.)

We should also be taking care not to savour any known corruption, or anything of the sort, which may get in the way of the Spirit's work of sanctification.

In these ways we ensure that the wounds of Calvary are indeed death to the 'old man' for us personally.

Part Two
THE TRUTH

7

WHY IS JESUS THE TRUTH?

If there is one single thing that is overwhelmingly attractive about the kingdom of God, and the faith that leads there, it is that it is the truth. The kingdom calls people to live within its walls simply because it is the truth. It is not merely another belief system, it is *the* truth. The King himself says, *"If anyone chooses to do God's will, he will find out whether my teaching comes from God or whether I speak on my own"* (John 7:17). *"If I am telling the truth, why don't you believe me?"* (John 8:46). *"If you hold to my teaching, you are really my disciples. Then you will know the truth, and the truth will set you free"* (John 8:31f). *"As it is, you are determined to kill me, a man who has told you the truth that I heard from God"* (John 8:40).

The only justification ever offered for the doctrine of Christianity and its kingdom is its truth. The whole teaching consists in recognising truth and following it, in a greater and greater realisation of truth and a closer and closer following of it in all our various and individual routes through life. There are no human acts or religious behaviour patterns laid down in Christianity which could possibly justify anyone, in the sense that we have been using the term, and save them from an otherwise inevitably ghastly eternal future. There is only the image of the truth who is Jesus Christ to guide us towards himself, and towards the establishment of the kingdom of God in us and around us. The fulfilment of this does not lie in a system of reward and punishment, depending on how well we adhere to the laws involved; it depends on our walking through the right gate, getting nearer to an inward imitation of Christ and an outer perfection in extending the kingdom of God. To affirm that is not to deny the reality of final judgement and the need at all times to abide in Christ, and going on believing in Jesus, and going on repenting.

Once through the gateway, assuming it is the correct one, the business of pressing on along the road of sanctification with this truth in our hands and hearts, as we have seen, is of enormous importance. Our greater or less blessedness in this life does not depend on the degree of perfection we reach on the way, but on the greater or less determination with which we pursue it.

Zaccheus's progression towards perfection, like that of the robber on the cross and the woman who was a sinner, is a greater state of blessedness than the unmoving, stagnant 'righteousness' of the Pharisee. The lost sheep is dearer than ninety-nine that were not lost in the first place. The story of the prodigal son, who was lost and found again, reminds us that we are dear and precious to God.

We have to keep moving. Blessedness is found in this 'moving' along the sanctifying road towards perfection, whereas standing still in any particular condition, for whatever reason, causes this state of blessedness to cease. So, kingdom seeker, *"Do not let your left hand know what your right hand is doing"* (Matthew 6:3). *"No one who puts his hand to the plough and looks back is fit for service in the kingdom of God"* (Luke 9:62). *"Do not rejoice that the spirits submit to you, but rejoice that your names are written in heaven"* (Luke 10:20). *"Be perfect, therefore, as your heavenly Father is perfect"* (Matthew 5:48).

But how can we confess to others that Christ is the truth? If we can find a proper and satisfying explanation for this, it will help us beyond measure in our attempts to become kingdom people.

So, in the first place, he is the Truth, as against those things which we now know to be shadows, and other versions of the truth under the law. Scripture says, *"The law was given through Moses; grace and truth came through Jesus Christ"* (John 1:17). *"These are a shadow of the things that were to come; the reality, however, is found in Christ."* (Colossians 2:17). The shadows are cast by the light but they are not the light. This holds true in every respect with regard to what follows. All these earlier shadows were signposts pointing to the Messiah. They were there to direct the children of Israel to look for Christ, the promised and anointed one. We can see that the law given to Moses was only a shadow of the good things to come. (See Hebrews 10:1 and Colossians 2:17.) Shadows were brought to an end in Jesus. By his coming to earth and carrying out his work, he put an end to the condemning power of all those laws which related only to him, and to what he had to do. Once the light itself had come, there was no longer any need for shadows. Thankfully, once through the gateway called 'justification', we all have the potential to be fulfilled in Christ, and whatever was originally displayed to the world in the shadows can be found completely in focus in him, in his light. In the Epistle to the Hebrews, the writer abundantly explains this to us, and Paul tells us in his letter to the Colossians that we are now complete in Christ, and consequently have no more need to follow any shadows. The kingdom seeker needs to avoid one already-mentioned, blackening and predominant shadow that lies across, strangles and suffocates the spiritual lives of many people. The shade cast by this error has caused many a Christian unwittingly to lose sight of the proper gateway, the proper road that leads on into the kingdom. There is, unhappily, and not for the first time, a 'Christ' preached from many pulpits who is slightly different from the one in the New Testament. Paul wrote to the Corinthians warning them about this wrongful identification which we, too, must guard against: *I hope you will put up with a little of my foolishness; but you are already doing that. I am jealous for you with a godly jealousy. I promised you to one husband, to Christ, so that I might present you as a pure virgin to him. But I am afraid that just as Eve was deceived by the serpent's cunning, your minds may somehow be led astray from your sincere and pure devotion to Christ. For if someone comes to you and preaches a Jesus other than the Jesus we preached, or if you receive a different spirit from the one you received, or a different gospel from the one you accepted, you put up with it easily enough* (2 Corinthians 11:1ff).

They had begun to follow a different 'Christ', one seeming very similar to the true Messiah but different in a number of important aspects. We have seen that it is important to look to Jesus as we travel the sanctifying way that leads deeper into the kingdom, but that sometimes proves problematic if identification of the leader is inaccurate. The devil is working, tirelessly and industriously, to lead our minds astray from a simple and pure devotion to Jesus Christ, and to a counterfeit instead. The enemy does this, sometimes quite successfully, by presenting us with three changes to fade our focus. They are:

1. An idea of Jesus which is slightly different to what is revealed in the New Testament. Many believers have been deceived about this; many are more familiar with a false picture of Jesus than with the real Jesus Christ. This is particularly true in the area of the supernaturally miraculous, some of the signs pointing to — and wonders of — the kingdom we are seeking. Only the true Lord Jesus Christ is reliable and consistent in answering prayer. Belief in what we might term an 'out-of-focus' picture of Christ is a major cause of the lack of miracles in the church today.

2. Some easily accept a different spirit, in place of the Holy Spirit whose work is authentically revealed in the New Testament. Many Christians are not familiar with the power of the Holy Spirit as

revealed to us in the Bible. We are to beware of what is counterfeit, and here the discernment of spirits is extremely important of course but, above all, we need a real understanding that the true Holy Spirit always glorifies Jesus and acts in ways that are revealed in God's Word.

3. Unless we check our scriptural sources carefully, it is easy to confuse a slightly different, attenuated version of the gospel with the full gospel. This slightly different but widely preached gospel has much less power. The healing of the sick and injured, and other miracle working, for example — multiple, everyday events in the kingdom — have been stripped away from it, giving us a message that no longer heals. This limited presentation of the gospel is the major reason for the wrong belief that eternal life and kingdom benefits begin only at our death.

The faithful may frequently be misled by theological ideas of the kingdom and of its King that originate in their teacher's own experiences of the Christian life rather than their devotion to the scriptures. Only the Christ of the New Testament is the Truth, the perfect image and reflection of the Father, not a shadow constructed out of our own philosophy and prayer life experiences.

Jesus is the true and practical fulfilment of all the prophecies of ancient times which testified to his character, nature, duties and offices, his work and his kingdom. Everything that was forecast in these prophecies was perfectly fulfilled in him, or was carried out by him, or will, in the due course of time, be accomplished by him. He is the great prophet discussed in Deuteronomy 18:15,18,19. The Jews themselves agreed with this in John 6:14, and all the prophets coming after Samuel spoke about him in this same light. (See Acts 3:22–24.)

We find the evangelists and apostles frequently applying the sayings and prophecies of the Old Testament to Jesus, and he himself recorded for us that the prophecy of Isaiah 61:1 was being fulfilled in him. (See Luke 4:18; see also 1 Peter 1:10–12.) And he addressed the two disciples on the road to Emmaus: *beginning with Moses and all the Prophets, he explained to them what was said about him in scripture.*

Jesus fully and faithfully completed every part of the work the Father sent him here to do. He was to bear our pain and to carry our sickness, and he did. He was to be wounded for our transgressions and bruised for our iniquities, and he was. The punishment that bought us peace was upon him, and by his stripes we were to be healed, and we are. (See Isaiah 53:5; Romans 4:25; 1 Corinthians 15:3 and 1 Peter 2:23.)

He offered himself to be an atoning sacrifice for our sins, the ultimate expression of everything he was sent to do, and he did it perfectly. Everything in his mission was completed, without anything being left out. In his prayer he could tell his Father that he had glorified him on earth, and had finished the work that he had been given to do; the Father was well pleased with him. (See John 17:4. See also Matthew 3:17; 12:18; 17:5; Mark 1:11 and Luke 3:22.) On the cross he was able to cry out in absolute truth, *"It is finished!"* (John 19:30).

He is the Truth, by which we mean a perfect example to everyone, with regard to the various duties and offices that he took on himself for our benefit.

He truthfully performed the office of a prophet, allowing his disciples to see the whole wisdom of God for the church. (See John 1:18; 15:15. See also in this context Ephesians 4:10–13; Acts 20:32; 1 Peter 1:10–12 and Hebrews 1:2.)

He also took on himself the office and work of a priest, offering himself as an all-embracing sacrifice. (See Hebrews 9:28 together with 2:17), becoming an everlasting priest, living for ever to intercede for us. (See Hebrews 7:25.)

As King, he calls a people to himself out of the world by his word and Spirit. (See Acts 15:14–16. See also Isaiah 55:4f and Psalm 110:3.) He brought into existence a visible church, a coming together of the faithful to profess his kingdom and declare his name, a body which he rules over because the government is on his shoulders. (See Isaiah 9:6f.) As King he is the head of the body, the church. (See Ephesians 1:22f and Colossians 1:18.) He fulfils his kingship even further by giving us grace (see Acts 5:3), rewarding us in our obedience (see Revelation 22:12), chastising the disobedient (see Revelation 3:19), and bringing his own people home, through all life's temptations and afflictions, overcoming all our enemies (see 1 Corinthians 15:25 and the whole of Psalm 110.) He continues his role as King in judging the living and the dead at the last day. (See 2 Thessalonians 1:8–9, Acts 17:31 and 2 Timothy 4:1.)

He is the Truth in that he completely satisfies every title and name given to him. He was called Jesus and he saved his people from their sins (see Matthew 1:21). He was called Christ, and he was anointed with the Spirit without measure (see John 3:34). He was set aside for his work, and filled with all power to effect it (see Job 6:27 and Matthew 28:18–20). He was set aside to be a prophet (see Acts 3:21f, Luke 4:18–21), a priest, as shown in Hebrews 4:14f; 5:5–7, and established as a king (see Psalm 2:6, Isaiah 9:6f, Matthew 21:5). He was called 'Emanuel' (see Isaiah 7:14), and was indeed God with us, being God and man in one person. He was called 'Wonderful' (Isaiah 9:6), and truly he was exactly that, in his two distinct natures in one person, at which thought even the angels wonder (see Ephesians 3:10f). He was called 'Counsellor', coming from heaven to earth from the Father's bosom, being familiar with and showing us the whole counsel of God with regard to our healing and salvation (see John 1:14–18; 3:13; 5:20; 15:15). He was called 'Lord' and 'God' and 'Messenger' in Psalm 110:1, Matthew 22:44, Psalm 45:6, Hebrews 1:8, Jeremiah 23:6 and 33:16, Malachi 3:1, Matthew 11:10, Psalm 83:18, Luke 1:76, John 1:1 and at many other points. He was also called 'everlasting Father' (see Isaiah 9:6); if we consider that expression to mean that

WHY IS JESUS THE TRUTH?

he is the author of eternal life, which he gives to everyone who believes in him, see John 6:39f,47,51; John 8:51, 10:28, 11:25f, Hebrews 5:9 and 7:25. Then he was called the 'Prince of Peace' (see again Isaiah 9:6), and indeed he is exactly that, being our peace (see Micah 5:5, Eph 2:14). He made peace between God and us, see Isaiah 53:5 and 53:19, Ephesians 2:17 and Colossians 1:20. Consequently, his gospel is known as the gospel of peace and his ministers are recognised as ambassadors of peace (see Isaiah 52:7, Romans 10:15, 2 Corinthians 5:19f, Ephesians 6:15). And he gives that peace, measured to be beyond all human understanding, to all his own kingdom dwellers (see Zechariah 9:10, John 14:27 and 17:33, Romans 5:1 and 14:17, 2 Thessalonians 3:17). Again, he was called the 'Lord our Righteousness' (Jeremiah 23:6,), and indeed he was, bringing in everlasting righteousness (Daniel 9:24) and, *It is because of him that you are in Christ Jesus, who has become for us wisdom from God —that is, our righteousness, holiness and redemption* (1 Corinthians 1:30), and, *God made him who had no sin to be sin for us, so that in him we might become the righteousness of God* (2 Corinthians 5:21).

He is the Truth resulting in and from the promises of God, which—

- Are all confirmed by him, and made 'yes' and 'Amen' in him. (See 2 Corinthians 1:20.)
- Point to him and centre around him as being the great promise himself.
- Are all based on his working for us as our only mediator between us and God in heaven.
- Are all given and distributed by him. (See John 14:13f.)

A further reason for our accepting him as being the Truth is that he amply answers and fulfils all the hopes and expectations of his people. He will never be found to lie to us, whatever

Satan may suggest, or our unbelieving hearts may prompt us to misconceive.

In the end, Christians will all find that he is indeed the truth without any argument, satisfying our proper, godly desires in his time, granting us everything that we could hope or expect from him. We will be completely filled to overflowing with seeing his likeness (see Psalm 17:15) and the abundance of his house (see Psalm 36:8), with his goodness (see Psalm 65:4) and with the richness of all his food (see Psalm 63:5).

We also call him the truth because he is the only road to divine healing and salvation because—

- The law of works cannot save us. (See Romans 8:3f.)
- Without Christ there is now no salvation to be had through the law of Moses. Those who have pursued a law of righteousness cannot attain it. Why not? —because they pursued it not by faith but as if it were by works. They stumbled over the stumbling stone. (See Romans 9:31f.) *Since they did not know the righteousness that comes from God and sought to establish their own, they did not submit to God's righteousness* (Romans 10:3).
- There is no healing and salvation to be gained through anything of a spiritual or philosophical nature that might be mixed in with our belief in Christ, as Paul fully explains in the letter to the Galatians.

In conclusion, Jesus Christ alone is the true, sure and safe provider of healing and salvation. Those kingdom seekers who follow the way, the truth and the life into the kingdom will not have got it wrong and they will not be disappointed. (See Isaiah 35:8.)

He is the Truth in the way that he leads and guides his people into the truth about God and the miraculous life in the kingdom. In this context he is called, *a teacher who has come from God* (John 3:2), and one that teaches, *the way of God in accordance with the truth* (Matthew 22:16). He was recognized as, *a prophet, powerful in word and deed before God and all the people* (Luke 24:19).

Lastly, he is upright and true in all his instruction in the gospel, and in all his works and actions in and about the company of his own people. All his offers, all his promises, all his instructions and commands, are done in the truth and uprightness of his love, his true tenderness and affection for his people, despite what any corrupting unbelief and jealousy might have thought and said to the contrary. And because he is the truth he must always be the same, unchanging in his love, whatever we might be misguided into thinking about him through our experiences of life. The kingdom seeker can rest assured that, Jesus being the truth, he is still today all that his Word says he is, and he always will be so.

8

GETTING OUR MINDS TO THINK TRUTHFULLY ABOUT GOD

This is a subject that can greatly trouble the kingdom seeker. We long to walk through life with our heads full of appropriate and suitable thoughts of God, but this often seems difficult. Surely we will only think rightly with the help of him who is the truth and came directly from the Father's heart. Looking for help in this matter, we will do well to remember these things—

1. Because of the Fall, human minds are naturally a mass of ignorance, lacking the wisdom of God. Our understanding is darkened (see Ephesians 4 17f), and it is quite natural for us to be in the darkness (see 1 John 2:9ff). We have been under the power of darkness (see Colossians 1:13) and, even worse, our minds are naturally filled with prejudice against God, through our naturally resident wickedness which is stirred up from time to time by the ruler of the kingdom of the air.

2. In this life, this evil thought pattern is only partially dealt with, even in the most godly. (See 1 Corinthians 13:12.)

3. The soul of the kingdom seeker may not be able to break through into a place of right and appropriate thinking, because of the continuous poisoning of some past and unconfessed corruption. We may even be in a place where, at best, we have collected some very narrow and unbiblical ideas about God and his ways; sometimes our thoughts are misty in their focus, if not altogether misshapen and blasphemous.

GETTING OUR MINDS TO THINK TRUTHFULLY ABOUT GOD

4. Another reason for our not having perfect thoughts of God is that we have not seen him, and cannot do so (see Matthew 11:27 and John 4:46). He is invisible (see 1 Timothy 1:17 and Hebrews 11:27). He, *alone is immortal and who lives in unapproachable light, whom no one has seen or can see. To him be honour and might forever. Amen* (1 Timothy 6:16). *No one has ever seen God; but if we love one another, God lives in us and his love is made complete in us* (1 John 4:12).

5. All we need in the way of saving knowledge of God can be found in Christ, who is *the radiance of God's glory and the exact representation of his being, sustaining all things by his powerful word* (Hebrews 1:3), and *the image of the invisible God* (Colossians 1:15). He is God incarnate, so that we can see in him what would otherwise be invisible to us.

6. If we want to see and know God, then we must go to Christ, who is the temple in which God dwells and manifests his glory. It is in and through him that we see and obtain our ideas about God. *For God, who said, "Let light shine out of darkness," made his light shine in our hearts to give us the light of the knowledge of the glory of God in the face of Christ* (2 Corinthians 4:6). Why in the face of Christ? —because it is by our faces that we are best known and most easily distinguished from other people. There is no other person than Christ through whom we can catch a glimpse of God.

So then, if we call on Christ to help us to break through to an appropriate view of God, and in order to have a suitable idea of his glory, we might consider the following things—

1. We would live our lives in wonder at the greatness of God, at the same time under the conviction of our own personal darkness and inability to picture him rightly, even after everything he has revealed about himself.

2. We should avoid attempting to discern God in nature. Anything that can be discovered about God through the study of creation

can be seen in Christ much more clearly. In our Lord we have a greater and more glorious discovery of God, and of his attributes, his justice, wisdom, power, goodness, holiness and truth.

3. *The grace of God that brings salvation has appeared to all men* (Titus 2:11). Grace appears in the gospel. Here we can see the special kindness and love of God towards man, which is only discovered in knowing Christ (see Titus 3:4). There we can find that manifold wisdom of God, that mystery hidden in God from the beginning of the world, that revelation that the principalities and powers in the heavenly realms must learn from the church which proclaims the gospel (see Ephesians 3:9f). Here in the gospel we find the forgiving of sinners and justice being done, all of which cannot be explained by nature. Nature alone cannot reveal the mystery of justice and mercy as it applies to the saving of a sinner —only the gospel can show that.

4. We go to Christ in the Gospels to find out about the Father. *"Anyone who has seen me has seen the Father"* (John 14:9). In particular, we must look into his face, the means by which he is recognised, the invaluable and glorious gospel. The gospel is his face. Here, in the gospel, God the Father is glorified in his Son, and in the healing and saving of sinners. The entire workload of salvation is placed on Jesus Christ, and the Father is glorified in him. So, in this gospel, we can see every line on the glorious face of Christ. It is in his face that we can see and discern the glory of God; it is in the gospel that we will get a good view of him. Every kingdom seeker who might long to come into a place of having right thoughts and perceptions of God must be well acquainted with the whole content of the gospel —well enough to see the character of Christ in every part of it.

5. In discovering all this, we must not go along this journey of unfolding awareness without our guide. Without him we may wander in the wilderness; the straight line voyage may turn out to be like a trip through a maze. We need to know Jesus is with

us all along; he will teach us to understand his own face, and to read the characteristics of glory to be seen there. He will act as our interpreter, teaching us how to understand what is written in the Bible. He is the one who gives the discerning eye and the understanding heart, together with the spirit of wisdom and understanding, that the seeker will need in order to take hold of the mysteries of God. We should also grasp firmly, by faith, the promises of the Spirit, making us spiritual and having our understanding enlightened more and more.

6. We must walk with godly awe and fear in all our journeying deeper into him. Our minds should be filled with thoughts of the majesty and glory of God. In this way we can walk humbly with him as we read about the glory of God in the face of Jesus Christ, this glorious gospel.

A word of caution may be appropriate, however. We have to accept that whilst God has revealed as much about his nature as we need to know, we cannot know everything about him. There is a warning in Job 11:7 not to set out to 'fathom the mysteries of God' nor 'probe the limits of the Almighty'. We should never forget that we cannot see him; and that we might not always keep hold of right and proper thoughts about him. This should keep us walking before him in awe and reverence, humbling ourselves in the dust, and keeping a sense of being in the presence of the one Almighty God whenever we make mention of his name. We should remind ourselves, when we begin to meditate on him, how great he is, and how dangerous it is to think wrongly of him, and how difficult it is to think appropriately about him.

Following these principles, the kingdom seeker will quickly learn to stay close to Jesus Christ and stay focused on right and proper thoughts about the heavenly Father, in line with the truth revealed in Holy scripture.

9

HOW TO GROW IN TRUTH, THE KNOWLEDGE OF GOD

Growing in the knowledge of Jesus Christ is a commanded duty (see 2 Peter 3:18), in the knowledge that he himself is eternal life (see John 17:3). Because our knowledge of him is shallow, we only know in part, the seeker will find that growing in this knowledge becomes increasingly desirable. *And we pray this in order that you may live a life worthy of the Lord and may please him in every way: bearing fruit in every good work, growing in the knowledge of God, being strengthened with all power according to his glorious might so that you may have great endurance and patience, and joyfully giving thanks to the Father, who has qualified you to share in the inheritance of the saints in the kingdom of light* (Colossians 1:10–12).

When justified by grace through faith, we are qualified to share in Christ's inheritance along with everyone else who lives in the kingdom. Grace and peace in abundance flow into our lives through our knowledge of God (see 2 Peter 1:2), so this knowledge must be added to and allowed to prepare the ground for Christian virtues to grow (see 2 Peter 1:5f). Realising this, the kingdom seeker cannot help but hunger after more and more of it, especially when he begins to feel the attraction of growing more into the image of his creator (see Colossians 3:10). It is only Christ the truth who can teach us here, *for God, who said, "Let light shine out of darkness," made his light shine in our hearts to give us the light of the knowledge of the glory of God in the face of*

Christ (2 Corinthians 4:6). The question then is: How do we obtain teaching from Jesus and acquire more of this truth about God?

Firstly, we should keep open a frame of mind that recognises our absolute need for Jesus to teach us. To maintain this hunger—

1. We should be aware of our ignorance, even when we know a great deal, or think we know a great deal, remembering that the best and most educated of us knows only in part (see 1 Corinthians 13:9). The kingdom seeker will soon realise that the greater the knowledge he manages to hold onto, the more he becomes aware of the chasm of ignorance that will appear to lie across his path.

2. The seeker should remember how deceitful the heart is, how proud and lazy. How ready it is to sit down and rest on a mere shadow of knowledge! *The man who thinks he knows something does not yet know as he ought to know* (1 Corinthians 8:2).

3. The kingdom seeker should search after this knowledge, knowing how absolutely necessary it is for kingdom walking with God, and kingdom convocation with others. It is this knowledge without sin that allowed Adam and Eve to feel at their ease, walking with God in the first kingdom on earth, the garden of Eden.

We should be convinced that we cannot gain this sort of knowledge through our own efforts, our own wisdom and intelligence. It needs the divine hand to write it into the seeker's soul. Through private study we may reach a level of literal, cerebral and speculative knowledge, which may well only serve to puff us up (see 1 Corinthians 8:1). If we gain it this way then we will never find this divinely inspired knowledge which is spiritual, hearty, practical and saving. We need the anointing here, which teaches us everything (see 1 John 2:27).

Moreover, there is a revealing of Christ in the Gospels which displays him convincingly as being fit and perfect for the role of teacher. The seeker should be looking at him as—

1. The substantial wisdom of the Father (see the whole of Proverbs chapter eight).

2. The one who is in the bosom of the Father (see John 1:18) and, consequently, sufficiently enabled and equipped to reveal the mysteries of God's heart to us.

3. Our go-between, who has the Spirit without measure, who teaches us (see John 3:34). He has hidden in him all the treasures of wisdom and knowledge (Colossians 2:3), and has dwelling in him all the fullness of God (see Colossians 1:19 and Isaiah 11:2; 61:1,2).

4. One who has the power to send the Holy Spirit, from whom comes the anointing that teaches us everything we need to know — and, *no lie comes from the truth* (1 John 2:21).

We should never forget his readiness to help us learn these things, and be encouraged by that thought to go forward. We should remember —

1. That his whole inclination is to help us by virtue of his position as a prophet, a witness, a leader and a commander of his people. (See Isaiah 55:4.)

2. That the Father has commissioned him for the purpose of teaching us and has sent him as 'a light to the Gentiles' (Isaiah 42:6; 49:6), and the Father is said to speak to us through him (see Hebrews 1:1f).

3. That he is already beginning this work in his followers by his Spirit. By that token he is prepared to finish it perfectly, for everything he does is perfect.

We should also remember the promises made to help us in our learning about Christ, such as in Habakkuk 2:14, *For the earth will be filled with the knowledge of the glory of the L*ORD*, as the waters cover the sea.* Isaiah 32:4 tells us that, *the mind of the rash will know and understand, and the stammering tongue will be fluent and clear*, and Jeremiah 31:34 proclaims that, *"No longer will a man teach his neighbour, or a man his brother, saying, 'Know the L*ORD*,' because they will all know me, from the least of them to the greatest," declares the L*ORD*."*

We must be on our guard against anything and everything within us that might stop our obeying the commanded duty of learning about God and therefore we should not—

1. Undervalue knowledge of his Word and his ways; for this will grieve him and be a hindrance.
2. Make the mistake of thinking that our philosophical speculation can add to his self-revelation. Intelligent deduction has little value when set against a clear and childlike gospel view of him.
3. Limit ourselves to a particular method of learning, or a particular time and style in which to do it.
4. Despise the day of small things, because the gains are small.
5. Be too curious where knowledge is not so important.

Whatever measure of knowledge we get, we should, in all haste, put it into practice, with humility and thankfulness, and set it to work. In this way it will increase as God gives us more. The honest and childlike kingdom seeker will find an urgent desire to share with others the gospel knowledge that God has revealed — like an enthusiastic student when first finding out something that may already be well known.

There should be a sensitivity, a vulnerability and openness to Christ's instructions, to the promptings of the Holy Spirit; and a greedy receiving, drinking in, and treasuring up in the soul of whatever he is pleased to infuse.

In all this, the disciple should watchfully guard against pride in the heart. *He guides the humble in what is right and teaches them his way* (Psalm 25:9).

Certainly, if this way of learning were followed more frequently and consistently, growth in knowledge of God through Christ would not be as rare as it is.

CAUTIONS

1. The seeker should never sit down to rest on any degree of understanding he may have reached, as if that is enough and as

if there were no need to move on. He should stay mindful of his duty of seeking, and pressing in for more.

2. Whenever he is giving this knowledge away, preaching, writing, discussing or teaching, he must keep his heart fixed on Christ. He should feel that he is acting as a brake on his own mouth as he waits for instruction, sending any number of sincere prayers to heaven, and checking what he thinks against the written Word of God, the Bible, to ensure that he only imparts the truth.

3. Beware of measuring growth in knowledge by growth in the ease of speaking and discussing any kingdom matter. Many people measure their knowledge by checking how fluently they can speak on a subject, or think they must not know very much because they cannot express it well. 'Knowledge' is measured by its agreement with the Word of God; how well it has been received is measured by the depth of impression that the truth has on the soul, and the changes it causes to the seeker's outlook on life.

4. Blessings abound to the seeker. (See Matthew 6:33). As the seeker's knowledge of Jesus grows, so will his trust in him. As trust grows, so will the daily number of miracles increase, and the Saviour is always to be thanked, praised and glorified for all fruit; the seeker will not take any personal credit for blessings given and received.

5. Beware of imagining that it might be possible to search out all there is to know about God. *"Can you fathom the mysteries of God? Can you probe the limits of the Almighty? They are higher than the heavens —what can you do? They are deeper than the depths of the grave —what can you know? Their measure is longer than the earth and wider than the sea"* (Job 11:7–9).

6. Beware, too, of imagining that it might ever be possible to plumb fully the depths of our own false and deceitful hearts. *The heart is deceitful above all things and beyond cure. Who can understand it?* (Jeremiah 17:9). It is God's prerogative to search and examine it. (See Jeremiah 17:10.)

7. Not every kingdom seeker will have the same level of knowledge. Everyone does not have the same capacity; differing capacities have been differently apportioned.

8. The ability to deduce and retain knowledge generally is something that can easily puff up a person. But the gift of knowledge, a spiritual gift from God, may open the eyes of the seeker even wider to the wonder of God.

9. We should not tempt the Lord, nor prescribe his methods for him. We would do much better standing at his door, listening to him than always calling for kingdom miracles. But of course there are moments when there is a prompting to ask him for a miracle. Many examples are seen in scripture, and we are always to be ready for his leading in this matter.

10

WHAT HELP IS THE TRUTH IN THE FACE OF OPPOSITION?

The kingdom seeker will be aware of needing the help of Jesus Christ the *truth* more than ever when kingdom work is challenged or overturned, when the truth about Jesus and the kingdom is condemned by others, and when the enemies of kingdom work seem to prosper in, and enjoy, their opposition to it.

The kingdom seeker is blessed in his seeking by many scriptural lessons concerning the kingdom of God, together with an urge to share them with other Christians. But imparting of such teaching to others will cause his enemies to rear up in his face. (See Matthew 10:34.) This is a very trying time. We are reminded of the writer of Psalm 73, who was made to stagger so much that he almost lost his foothold, and his feet had nearly slipped from under him. He was on the point of regretting ever having been a godly person, saying in verse 13,

> *Surely in vain have I kept my heart pure;*
> *in vain have I washed my hands in innocence.*

He is wondering if his whole devotion has been wasted time. We wonder whether perhaps it was such a situation that was the occasion of Jeremiah remarking, in 8:18, *O my Comforter in sorrow, my heart is faint within me.* And in v. 20 is written, *The harvest is past, the summer has ended, and we are not saved.* Earlier, in v. 15, we read, *We hoped for peace but no good has come, for a time of healing but there was only terror.* Now the seeker's only real hope in this situation has to be the Rock of Ages, Jesus the truth. It is he alone who can keep his back straight and upright on such shaking and reeling occasions. To the soul of a kingdom seeker shaken in such a time of trial, the presence of Jesus Christ will be the only support available.

But the question before us is this: How should kingdom seekers make use of the riches of their inheritance in Christ in times like this? How can we be kept strong enough not to faint and succumb to the thrashing of such storms? It will help us to remember certain things:

1. Christ is frequently referred to as being the Father's servant in all this magnificent work of redemption. (See Isaiah 42:1, 49:3–6; 52:13 and 53:11, together with Zechariah 3:8.) It follows from these readings that this work has been entrusted to him, and he stands with the kingdom seeker in the middle of the fury. He is to finish the work. *On him God the Father has placed his seal of approval* (John 6:27), and he often tells us himself that he has been 'sent' by the Father. (See John 4:34, 5:23f, 30, 36f; John 6:38–40, 44, 57, and John 8:16,18.)

2. While he was with us in the flesh, Jesus finished every piece of work that was committed to him here, having bought all that was planned to be bought with his blood, paying the price demanded by justice. (See John 17:4 and 19:30.) In doing this he bought a people for himself. (See Revelation 5:9 and Luke 1:68.) His work is a purchased work, bought with blood; the kingdom seeker has the huge privilege of entering into the kingdom life which flows from that finished work of Jesus.

3. His resurrection is undoubted proof that justice is done, and that the punishment has been exacted. His ascension to the Father's right hand can be taken as the next heaven-intended step towards

the eventual defeat of all his enemies and that his work of truth will flourish. The Father said to him:

> *"Sit at my right hand*
> *until I make your enemies a footstool for your feet."*
> See Psalm 110:1

Therefore God exalted him to the highest place and gave him the name that is above every name, that at the name of Jesus every knee should bow, in heaven and on earth and under the earth, and every tongue confess that Jesus Christ is Lord, to the glory of God the Father (Philippians 2:9–11).

4. Today it is as true as it always was that Christ has the power to carry on with his work of growing the kingdom. All authority in heaven and earth has been given to him (see Matthew 28:18), and every knee must bow to him (see Philippians 2:10). All judgement has been given to him (see John 5:22, 27); angels, powers, and authorities are placed under his control (see 1 Peter 3:22). How, then, can his work fall short? Who could possibly succeed in preventing the light of the kingdom, already beginning to shine through the believer, from lighting the world?

5. Christ uses the kingdom seeker as one in whom others might see something of his kingdom. Many of these storms are caused by enquirers holding the telescope to the eye the wrong way around, causing the object in view to appear relatively unimportant, insubstantial and open to easy criticism. They treat the kingdom seeker in his kingdom proclamations as being of little value, as they cannot see and understand what is being proclaimed.

6. Christ has set out to finish the work he has begun. He has all creation at his command. He is about the business of perfecting the application (of extending the kingdom), just as he has already perfected the purchasing of the people to populate it. The kingdom

seeker may rest assured that Christ will never leave the battlefield (see Exodus 17:8–13).

7. Jesus Christ will, eventually be *glorified in his holy people* (2 Thessalonians 1:10). Then everyone will clearly see whose wisdom is true, his or that of mankind —and whose work has flourished.

8. This is the way of things: that anyone manifesting Christ in the authority that he has in his kingdom over the things of Satan may have much snatched away from him by the dragon. However, whatever the battle, God will keep in eternal life those who, going on believing in Jesus, faithfully proclaim the kingdom, walk in obedience, and repent as often as necessary of sins committed.

Some cautionary things need to be added here, to make the very best of every difficult and stormy situation.

1. Our understanding of all these things we have mentioned should never allow us to slacken our application and watchfulness in prayer. Properly understood, they should act as a spur in our side to set us in forward motion again, rather than being a bridle to hold us steady and stationary.

2. Do not think that Christ's work is losing ground, even when it seems so to us on such stormy occasions. He may well be breaking down part of his work in order to rebuild it more gloriously. *O afflicted city, lashed by storms and not comforted, I will build you with stones of turquoise, your foundations with sapphires. I will make your battlements of rubies, your gates of sparkling jewels, and all your walls of precious stones* (Isaiah 54:11f). His work will soon be prospering again, built on a better foundation.

3. Always be wary of one particular and common human failing: we are inclined to judge situations by rules of our own making, and not by the rule of truth. This is how we can often be mistaken. Kingdom seekers should avoid walking too much by commonsense and too little by faith. If we walk in line with fleshly 'sense', we judge in sense, and consequently are often

wrong. These wrong judgements dishonour God and sadden our own hearts.

4. We should not conclude that the purposes of the kingdom are ruined and lost, if only temporarily, because those who would oppress it seem to be winning in one particular corner of the world. The work of kingdom building is seen in many of the churches around the world. If his kingdom grows and prospers in some other place in the world, we must surely go on proclaiming that his kingdom is coming!

5. We must be careful not to think badly of this work of kingdom seeking and sharing because it is sometimes quite a jolting ride. We are not acquainted with the depths of the King's infinite wisdom; we cannot see the road ahead as he does. We are sometimes guilty of thinking that he ought to ride smoothly, fast and triumphantly along the road. But this is fleshly judgement, made by someone unacquainted with the wonderful and glorious plans which God has. It is Christ himself, at the heart of his kingdom, who is the stumbling block for many who would throw accusations at the kingdom seeker. It is the accusers who are in danger.

6. We should be careful not to think that the King might have forgotten the work of extending the kingdom because some of our prayers about the work have seemingly not been answered. He may indeed be getting on with the work and taking other routes than those prescribed for him by the kingdom seeker!

7. We should beware of becoming despondent, losing heart when we see few other saints joining in the work of seeking and extending the kingdom. The truth is that the Lord does not need man's help to carry on this work; he might drive it by his own Spirit instead, although he sometimes thinks it good to honour some of us by making us instruments for pressing the kingdom forward. Nor should we think either that the kingdom cannot advance because someone is standing against it, nor because those who should be involved in it and belonging to it are fainting by the wayside.

WHAT HELP IS THE TRUTH IN THE FACE OF OPPOSITION?

Without warning, a furious storm came up on the lake, so that the waves swept over the boat. But Jesus was sleeping. The disciples went and woke him, saying, "Lord, save us! We're going to drown!"

He replied, "You of little faith, why are you so afraid?" Then he got up and rebuked the winds and the waves, and it was completely calm.

Matthew 8:24 – 26

11

TRUTHS TO BE DISCOVERED ALONG THE WAY

It must be the constant desire of the kingdom seeker to have an enlarged heart's view of the kingdom. A small view will only allow the benefits of a small kingdom; the larger and more encompassing the view, the greater the variety of enjoyments and benefits that can be had there. Like Jabez, we should be crying out to the God of Israel, *"Oh, that you would bless me and enlarge my territory!"* (1 Chronicles 4:10).

An enlarging vision of the kingdom will cause the seeker to want to pass on to others the truths of the Word. This desire should be allowed expression as opportunities arise as wisdom and understanding increase.

While all this should be a matter for constant prayer, we need to remember some basic points. It is not given to everyone to obtain a complete view of the beauty and scope of the kingdom. Only by deliberately approaching the subject with a child's purity of heart and poverty of spirit will the eye of the heart be uncluttered enough to catch a glimpse of it (see Matthew 5:2,3,8 and Mark 10:13–16). The kingdom seeker must be prepared to accept that much of what has been learned before first setting out on the kingdom road may now be like a cataract that clouds the eye and the vision before him. If necessary, he may have to be prepared to submit that former 'understanding' for breaking down and remoulding by the Holy Spirit. Many misguided souls will attempt to blunt the cutting edge of discovery by insisting that any growth of knowledge must necessarily come out of what has been learned before. This approach is used to justify theologically where they have been. Many believers measure heresy in this way. To be beguiled by this apparently sound piece of logic is to be tempted off the right road and into a clogging sea of philosophy. The logic of always following on from what has gone before only holds water if the earlier ground covered was itself true kingdom territory. Christ, on his part, did not encourage us to think that knowledge of the kingdom grows from the current place of understanding. Rather, he taught us to adopt an attitude of readiness to begin again. When he taught the kingdom to the church he told them, *"Repent, for the kingdom of heaven is near"* (Matthew 4:17). And, in reply to Nicodemus, Jesus declared, *"I tell you the truth, no one can see the kingdom of God unless he is born again"* (John 3:3). (See also 1 Peter 1:23.) That is a statement about the new beginning at the start of Christian life, the new birth. We must be prepared to lay everything down (and that includes our preconceived notions of the kingdom) in order to follow him into his kingdom. *"It is easier for a camel to go through the eye of a needle than for a rich man to enter the kingdom of God"* (Matthew 19:24). Earlier, in Matthew 19:21 Jesus had told a rich young man, *"If you want to be perfect, go, sell your possessions and give to the poor, and you will have treasure in heaven. Then come, follow me."* It might be that only a little kingdom living can as yet be discerned in the seeker. Kingdom growth takes time and the seeker might be anywhere along the path. It is important to allow time for application and for God's work in us to grow and flourish. *"The kingdom of heaven is like a mustard seed, which a man took and planted in his field. Though it is the smallest of all your seeds, yet when it grows, it is the largest of garden plants and becomes a tree, so that the birds of the air come and perch in its branches"* (Matthew 13:31f). Things do take time.

The seeker should diligently study the character of Jesus in the Gospels. The Bible leads us to look at Jesus. Through him alone we can come into a new relationship as adopted children of the Father. The kingdom seeker should keep the Bible close to hand, knowing that it is God's precious written Word, his final self-revelation, teaching us his ways, his will and his purposes; it is beyond all price; it is to be read, learnt, taken into the heart and mind, transforming our understanding and our will. The study of the words and works of Christ, and consequently the study of the will and character of Jesus, is vital: without it the kingdom seeker will not move forward into the kingdom. This is because —

1. The kingdom is wherever God's will is the will of those who live in it. It is therefore not something that can be appreciated unless we understand the beauty of the Father's will. We cannot become part of the kingdom unless we, too, have the Father's will in our hearts.

2. We have been sent Jesus, so we are to grow in our understanding of the things of the kingdom. Colossians 1:10ff tells us that Jesus is the *image of the invisible God*. Later we read that, *in Christ all the fullness of the Deity lives in bodily form* (2:9).

3. The first article of the Christian faith must be exuberantly upheld. It is the confession that man has one, and only one, true object of worship. There is one holy God, Creator of heaven and earth. He is Lord, Saviour and healer. We are beholden to him for our life, all its meaning, and all its hope. Worshipping our one God means that anything else we put in the place of our loyalty to God through Jesus Christ is an idol. We may be idolaters if we ascribe ultimate value (worship) to national power, racial prestige or financial success, cultural or denominational tradition, church rank (or even our own theological ideas). Above all, of course, we must affirm and worship (give worth to) *only* the one true God, not any other deities or images of deities.

4. Failure in those areas may pull the seeker backwards and

further from the centre of the kingdom which has the crucified Christ at its heart. For the kingdom seeker to begin and continue in commitment to the one true Lord Jesus Christ is, as we have noted, to refuse to have any other gods at all. Various ideas about the will and intentions of the Lord exist around the church in confusing profusion, as do disciples' personal interests, worship styles, agendas, programmes, and loyalties to particular church organisations. But these are not to be put in the place that belong to God alone; they do not save us or heal us.

Again, we remind ourselves that the close study of the will of the Son will give a closer understanding of the will of the Father. As the seeker then bends his own will to conform to the Father's will, so he becomes absorbed increasingly into the life of the kingdom. The kingdom is manifested increasingly through the seeker's life and ministry, and he himself lives increasingly in the beauty of the Father's will.

The kingdom seeker must be prepared for his heart attitudes and his ministry to undergo a degree of change. These things will be affected by what is found in the kingdom.

The kingdom seeker must keep a proper awareness of his own responsibility in the matter of kingdom spreading. God reminds us that his word is designed to be carried into the world in our hearts and on our lips as we proclaim the good news of the death and resurrection of Jesus and the call to repentance and faith in him. Proclamation is not of rituals, theories or our own pretensions.

With respect to kingdom ministry, the truths to be discovered in the kingdom can be ministry transforming. How else could it be possible that we flawed and fallible people of God, the way we are as human beings, can exercise Christ's astonishing ministry in the kingdom?

1. If Jesus Christ, his finished work and sacrifice, do not result in the seeker becoming more like him, then the walk of the seeker could be said to be failing. Insofar as the seeker is concerned,

Christ's life and death would effectively have been thrown away. Jesus' death for us on Calvary changes the way we relate to people and the world. The penitent believer's justification by grace through faith, does not mean that we are free to go on living the same kind of life as others, following the same selfish interests and desires that others have. That would be a vain, fleshly, arrogant dream. The crucified Christ at the centre of his kingdom signifies a new way of living life.

2. Seeing kingdom truths and comparing them with 'real' life experience means that many matters arise that require much attention, study and meditation on the Word on the part of the kingdom seeker. For example, in John 14:12, Jesus tells us a kingdom truth. He says that, *"Anyone who has faith in me will do what I have been doing. He will do even greater things than these, because I am going to the Father."* Taken in context, Christ is discussing his miraculous works, the healing of the sick and the casting out of demons —all kingdom work. Such things may be manifested in the life of the kingdom seeker as the Holy Spirit acts. *Then the disciples went out and preached everywhere, and the Lord worked with them and confirmed his word by the signs that accompanied it* (Mark 16:20); and, *"How great are his signs, how mighty his wonders! His kingdom is an eternal kingdom; his dominion endures from generation to generation"* (Daniel 4:3); *They will speak of the glorious splendour of your majesty, and I will meditate on your wonderful works* (Psalm 145:5). And yet, among believers today, there are few who are manifesting the truth of these things in their lives.

3. The seeker's attitude to things which are hard to comprehend will begin to change as he lives longer in the kingdom and is affected by it. For example, it is a kingdom truth that Christ healed every sick person who trusted enough to ask him for that healing. The experience of the church at prayer is that this happy state has not been continued. As God is love and truth and does

not change over time, and as Christ is the perfect image of the Father, the seeker will have to search to understand this apparent change. The ordinary believer ignores this anomaly and, when faced with having to address the paradox, will begin to tear down the kingdom truth. The seeker, however, will begin to bear up under the same kingdom truth, and consequently will begin to realize its truth in his own life and ministry.

4. The greater reason for the miraculous gifts appearing to be withdrawn from the daily lives of believers and yet restored in the daily lives of kingdom seekers is that simple expectancy, trust and a thirst for personal holiness have been, to a large extent, lost. Dry believers may soon begin to mock whatever experiences of the kingdom and gifts of the Spirit they have not experienced for themselves. They begin to tear them all down, giving the impression that they must be some kind of make-believe. The kingdom seeker may care to stop here for a moment and ask himself, 'Why am I not as able to work miracles as regularly and reliably as the early Christians did?' The seeker's own heart should say that it is not through any ignorance or inability, but purely because he never thoroughly intended it. Such a kingdom life has perhaps never been sought, but the door is opened in the seeking (see Revelation 3:20, concerning the change that can occur if a church member opens the door to Jesus).

5. Here is a key biblical truth that relates directly to the kingdom. Christ is the radiance of the Father's glory, the exact representation of his being. When we are in Christ, walking obediently according to his word, repenting of sin and continuing in faith, he can use us powerfully in witness.

In Genesis 1:26 it is recorded that God said, *"Let us make man in our image, in our likeness, and let them rule over the fish of the sea and the birds of the air, over the livestock, over all the earth, and over all the creatures that move along the ground."* The kingdom seeker should become increasingly aware, as he dwells in the kingdom, that he has been created to exercise the kingdom on earth. He has been created to be responsible for the outworking, the exercise of tilling the ground, in the kingdom growing on earth. Kingdom seekers have been brought into the kingdom to be his ambassadors. God has entrusted kingdom work on earth to human beings, who need the constant help, guidance and wisdom that the Holy Spirit can continue to release to those who love and obey Jesus.

CAUTION

1. Adam could have remained firmly rooted in the kingdom if he had so wished; he fell because of his own will. It was because his will was soft and capable of being bent back and forth – and because he lacked the determination to persevere – that he fell so easily. His choice between good and evil was a free one.

2. Peter could have stood firm on the surface of the water for very much longer, had he not taken his eyes off Jesus and begun to watch the waves of the stormy world again.

Part Three
THE LIFE

12

WHY IS JESUS CHRIST CALLED THE LIFE?

Even those who might appear to be the holiest folk in the land may still not really be enjoying the wonderful life of the kingdom. Many are missing out. And we may find the lowliest of human beings seated at the kingdom banquet top table. Jesus Christ, who is 'the life', can lift a believer and place him where he will.

The scriptural truths we have noticed in this book thus far (and please compare and check carefully for yourself all that you read here and elsewhere against the pure teaching of the Bible) should have taught us very clearly one great truth: we are to live and abide in Jesus Christ. Moreover, with his life operating within us, we are to come to live and work in his kingdom.

The kingdom seeker cannot rely for his entry key on a life's commitment to the church and its ministry, nor to a lifetime of good works, nor to being Christian by 'nature' nor on having submitted himself correctly to church procedures and ordinances. The only way into the kingdom is Jesus Christ himself, the truth —and only he is the life to be had there.

There are four points of truth to be addressed here.
1. Our situation is that we all need Jesus desperately because without him in reality we have no spiritual life, only some poor substitutes, delusions or counterfeits instead.

2. There is no other way to obtain a supply of true spiritual life other than through him. He is the **only** life. Full and active membership of our favourite organisation, club, church or political party, is a deceiving bed to lie on, as is any other religion. It cannot fill us with the truth about life. Utter devotion to a career may give the impression of being the fulfilling life, but it is a poor thing in comparison with a life in kingdom riches.

3. Kingdom walking, this completely different and satisfying life, can be had fully and completely in Jesus. Not only is he able to sharpen our outlook on every aspect of life, he is the life itself.

4. Learning to bring the kingdom close to those who have need of it becomes a most satisfying outreach because it is the undiluted work of Christ.

These four points should be of vital interest to all kingdom seekers. This is because all of us, by our nature and inclination, were dead in our sins. We needed to be made alive, a new creation. Christ is indeed that life, the one that we can have instead of being legally under the sentence of death for Adam's transgression (see Romans 5:15) and for that original corruption of heart we have all inherited.

The sentence of the law has been partially executed in both the body and the soul. As far as the body is concerned, it is now subject to death and all its forerunners: stress, pains, sickness, all kinds of fear, worry, relationship breakdowns and much more. As far as the soul is concerned, in its natural, fallen state it is also dying in many different ways. It may die by way of being apart from God and it may die from sin. In both cases, those death pains may be manifested in the present or the future. We remind ourselves again of man's natural state:

1. Separated from God and from his favour. (See Genesis 3:8,10,24.)

2. It is as though we are under God's curse and anger; it would be sheer folly to deny that, by nature, we were children of wrath

(see Ephesians 2:2,5), and servants of Satan (2 Timothy 2:26). It is true that we cannot please God until we are brought out of this condition. Even our ordinary and everyday actions are considered sin (see Proverbs 21:4). Our religious activities, whether instituted by the church on our behalf, or carried out on our own accord, apart from Jesus Christ and his kingdom, are useless or misleading, suggesting to us that we are operating in obedience to him, whereas the opposite may be true. Will this include even our prayers (see Proverbs 28:9), all our ways (see Proverbs 15:9) and all our thoughts and purposes (see Proverbs 15:26)? As to God's judgement in the future, it will be everlasting excommunication from his presence, and from the glory of his power (see 2 Thessalonians 1:8f). It would mean being placed in submission to hell's torturers (see Mark 9:44,46,48).

The spiritual condition of those who live outside the kingdom life in Jesus Christ is lamentable! If only they could see and feel it! Many believers understand by all this that they are saved by leading a full Christian life of prayer and worship, by reading the Bible and by appreciating fine speaking which, by and large, agrees with what they already understand by Christianity. Even all this is not kingdom living. Kingdom living is living in Jesus Christ the Saviour himself. He is the life; he motivates and gives life to the kingdom seeker.

We have alluded to the sad condition of those whose hearts are far from the kingdom, who in their lives do not acknowledge, or believe in and worship, Jesus crucified and risen, true God and true man. Unhappily, people do not realise; they do not think about it, they do not believe it, they do not feel it, they cannot see it. What is the result of this ignorance? Firstly, they cannot lament their own condition and therefore cannot be humbled in it. Secondly, they cannot, and will not, search for a remedy; for those of us who think we are well do not bother finding a doctor. If we allow our minds to dwell a little while on this situation, would we not all set out to search again for that gate of justification, if we have not yet found the kingdom life? Would we not surely want to leave behind everything which has been hindering us?

I can only ask every believer to consider these things:

1. Whether or not the voice of Christ, which can raise the dead, has been both heard and welcomed in their soul. This is a potent calling.

2. Whether or not a noticeable and thorough change in the soul took place while entering through the gate of justification, a change that runs through the whole person so that all becomes new. (See 2 Corinthians 5:17.)

3. Whether or not there has grown up an awareness of the new life within, and a consciousness of being led by the Spirit.

4. Whether or not there is a deep desire to live to the glory of the Lord Jesus, the Redeemer.

It is heartbreaking to think how people in a condition of 'lostness' are so unwilling to come out of that state; how unwilling they are to suspect their own spiritual condition, or to consider that it might not be right with God, and that they, as yet, may be not fully converted. How unwilling they are to sit down and try to seriously examine their own spiritual life against the touchstone of the Word of God. How unwilling they are to hear anything that might wake them up, or suggest that there might be any deadness in their condition. How ready they are to stifle the challenges of kingdom conversation or any movement of the Spirit in their conscience which tends to alarm their soul. How badly they speak about those ministers who teach kingdom truths —which serve to make them jealous and set them to thinking in challenging ways about their own salvation.

This should put all of us to thinking deeply about what it is that lies at the centre of our lives, and what it is that brings us peace and quiet when thoughts of unfulfilled ministry, death, judgement, hell, and the wrath of God creep up on us and trouble our souls.

WHY IS JESUS CHRIST CALLED THE LIFE?

If it is anything other than Christ that our soul tends to lean on, and derive its comfort from, then we are bound to meet eventually with a tragic disappointment.

The kingdom seeker needs to be sure then, that the heart renounces all ways and means of strengthening, and of escaping eternal death, other than Jesus, who is the resurrection and the life. He alone is the life and is called *the bread of life* (John 6:35,48). He is also called *"The resurrection and the life"* (John 11:25) and the *water of life* (Revelation 21:6 and 22:17). Scripture also refers to the *tree of life* (Revelation 22:2,14), and the leaves of the tree are for the healing of the nations. Jesus is also called the *author of life* (Acts 3:15). Being the perfect life, he is willing to help us and to deliver us from death—

1. He delivers us from the judgement sentence of the law (see Romans 5:17,18), taking on our behalf the curse of the law, becoming sin for us (see 2 Corinthians 5:21).

2. He takes away the curse and sting of things going wrong, even death itself, causing everything to work together for good for those who love God (see Romans 8:28). He has dealt the devil a mortal blow (see Hebrews 2:14), and the sting of death is taken away, see (1 Corinthians 15:56f).

3. He is relied on, in the kingdom, to deliver from the power of sin and corruption (see Romans 7:24) and from all those spiritual strokes of the heart —spiritual blindness and hardness of heart being two examples.

4. He is relied on in the kingdom to deliver us from all sickness and injury to our minds and bodies (see Isaiah 53:5, Matthew 8:16f and 1 Peter 2:24). It is sad that so many continue to ignore the fountain of living water, and dig broken cisterns for themselves which cannot hold any amount of water for any time at all.

Here we can identify three further points of truth. Firstly, even kingdom seekers need Christ to be life to them, because they have their fits of deadness. If this were not the case, why would Christ have told believers that he was the life? Everyday experience abundantly confirms it, in that—

1. We are sometimes weak and unable to resist temptation, or to go about any commanded duty, as if we are somehow quite devoid of any energy, quite dead.

2. Because of the opposition we often meet from all sides, we can easily be affected by discouragement. It becomes a great temptation to avoid situations of potential confrontation.

3. We have great need of Christ to rebuild and enliven us continuously when, through daily fighting against evil things, we become weary and faint-hearted. *He gives strength to the weary and increases the power of the weak* (Isaiah 40:29).

4. We are as capable as anyone of falling ill and need to breathe the restoring atmosphere of the kingdom.

In many such ways as this the seeker may sometimes feel weak and dispirited along the way, but God deals graciously and encouragingly with those who seek him, keeping us humble in the knowledge that we are spiritually destitute creatures, needing daily injections of the life. We are continually built up so that we can run many errands for him who is the life. In this way we have a great deal to do with him and remain in great need of him. He can show himself to be wonderful, in us and through us, and we see his skill in 'raising' the dead. We can be taught more and more about the life of faith and of depending on him, and be trained up in that style of life. More and more people will acknowledge and recognise him, submitting to him as sovereign God, doing his will here on earth —as it is done in heaven.

The kingdom seeker's low points are not known to everyone, and neither does everyone know what lies sometimes in the heart. Many Christian believers deceive themselves into thinking that living in the kingdom is an easy life but the righteous are strengthened through many persecutions and what may sometimes feel like the hardest trials. Throughout such trials, the seeker's

WHY IS JESUS CHRIST CALLED THE LIFE?

natural reaction is one of praise for the wisdom, faithfulness and power of God. It is God who brings the broken ship through so much broken water; and we thank him for his goodness. He allows us to learn to be dependent on him.

We must learn from this journey that nothing without Christ will help fill our hunger and our weariness: not even prayer, reading, hearing, meditation, attending sermons, lectures and conferences. Some of these things may provide some discipline, but help is not to be found in them. Only Jesus himself is the life.

What we might call 'extraordinary' religious activities — like fasting and vows — will never revive a fainting or a sickly soul. They are not Christ, and they are not the life.

A stout and courageous heart is not enough on its own to strengthen the seeker. If he who is the Life does not breathe, everything will melt away.

When the seeker has been walking in the kingdom for a while, there will have built up a stock of established grace which remains in the soul. This will not be sufficient to revive the sick soul, if the Life does not breathe on it. We need the constant in-filling of the Holy Spirit.

It would be good if all believers lived every day in awareness of these truths and declared publicly that there is no other way through life than to go on receiving it from him who is the life itself.

This stock of reviving strength is more than generously conveyed to his children, and on the easiest of terms.

A simple request for strengthening help is always granted so that—

1. The poor will see and be glad —you who seek God, may your hearts live! (Psalm 69:32).
2. Those who know Jesus as their Saviour and Lord will not miss life (see John 17:3 and 1 John 5:20).
3. If we will go on repenting and believing and trusting in him and

relying on him, we go on having eternal life in him (see John 3:15f, 36, and also 6:40,47). We can also see this in 1 Timothy 1:16.

4. If we will come to him (see John 5:40), and cast the dead parts of our life on him, we shall live.

5. If we will hear his voice (see Isaiah 55:3) and take hold of his instructions, we shall live, because they are the instructions of life.

6. Even if the believer considers himself spiritually dormant and unable to make the kingdom journey, merely looking towards him again will give strength and life to the spirit (see Isaiah 45:22).

7. If the soul is so weak that it cannot even look, but is still willing, he will still come with the free gift of the water of life, (see Revelation 22:17). And the water of life is Christ himself.

Everything in Christ contributes to this kingdom life and the strengthening of the saints who would live there. His words and doctrine are the words of eternal life (see John 6:63, 68 and Philippians 2:16).

His works and ways are the ways of life (see Acts 2:28). His character, his saving acts in redemption, his suffering, miracle working and everything he did and does for us as Intercessor, add to the enlivening of the seeking soul.

13

CAN THE LIFE HELP US TO MOVE ON?

Sometimes the believer is so locked into what has been learned in the past — perhaps he has always understood himself to live in the kingdom — that he can no longer discern any difference between his own calling and living in that kingdom. He thinks of 'works', for example, as being things that pour from his faith and which are helpful to others, whereas we learn from Christ that the definition is much more specific than that: work is the proclamation of the kingdom and the doing of deeds of a miraculous nature that pour out of a kingdom life. Jesus told his disciples, *"My Father is always at his work to this very day, and I, too, am working"* (John 5:17) and again, *"Don't you believe that I am in the Father, and that the Father is in me? The words I say to you are not just my own. Rather, it is the Father, living in me, who is doing his work"* (John 14:10). And the apostle longed for us all to have the Spirit of wisdom and revelation, so that we might know him better (see Ephesians 1:17). He goes on to pray, in verse 18, that the eyes of his readers would be enlightened so that they might realize the hope to which they have been called, the riches of the Lord's glorious inheritance prepared for us, and his incomparably great power for those who believe. He prays for the spirit of revelation to open our eyes to the rich benefits of kingdom living and the supernatural power that awaits us there.

However, the believer may himself be under such a stifling

weight of theological concrete, and erroneous ideas about the kingdom, that little or no difference can be seen between him and others. He may even become sceptical about the things of the kingdom. So how can we invite Christ to help us throw off this heavy blanket of rigid unbelief about the kingdom that prevents the believer from any innocent and childlike exploration of this mysterious territory?

We need to think about how such a smothering situation arose in the first place; how Jesus can be life to the soul under these circumstances, and how the believer might gain his help to move into kingdom living. The sad situation we are considering may have arisen from an abusive situation around the believer at a time when the heart was particularly vulnerable, thus surprising and overpowering the soul. Through sleight of hand, Satan can 'steal' all the childlike inquisitiveness away from the believer who is not watchful enough, and, little by little, as it were, send him to sleep. Through carelessness in missing the first signs of this, the believer unwittingly allows its growth. The most common and early signs are the replacing of a sense of spiritual adventure with a growing desire for the ritualistic or for just the pastoral expression of ministry. Another sign of this sleep is that the believer dismisses any teaching which is not confirmed by what he has learned before. This deadness of the believer's sense of adventure may have arisen because of wrestling in his mind over things of relative spiritual insignificance. So he becomes less sensitive in matters of much greater importance, like the soul's salvation and the hunt for the kingdom. Unable to stir himself and shake off that spiritual laziness and sleepiness, he finds that along comes yet another snooze, and another sleep, and a spiritual folding of the hands across the stomach, to prepare for yet more comfortable slumber instead of adventure.

Continuing in a known sin, willingly or unwillingly, without repenting of it, might have brought on and sustained this spiritual

CAN THE LIFE HELP US TO MOVE ON?

illness, as it did with King David. One common sin is jealousy of those who may already display such gifts and graces as are freely available in the kingdom. The display of this jealousy normally takes the form of a readiness to tear down kingdom principles rather than explore them with a childlike and inquisitive nature.

How can Christ bring life to the soul under these circumstances? He can indeed be that re-invigorating life simply because God keeps possession of the soul. The seed remains in the soil, the root anchors itself firmly in the ground. There is still life in the heart. Although there may be no longer any sign of it, the word is not dead. *"As the rain and the snow come down from heaven, and do not return to it without watering the earth and making it bud and flourish, so that it yields seed for the sower and bread for the eater, so is my word that goes out from my mouth: It will not return to me empty, but will accomplish what I desire and achieve the purpose for which I sent it"* (Isaiah 55:10f).

In due time God may waken the believer's soul and raise him out of this spiritual lethargy. He may do this either by persuading the believer to accept judgement from another, as in the case of David; or through the dispensation of his tenderness and mercy, as in the case of Peter.

God sometimes allows us to discover something of our own spiritual reluctance by giving enough knowledge and commonsense, and by sending enough light for the soul to see for itself that it is not well. Sometimes he wakens the soul to kingdom adventure by making it freshly aware that Jesus is the life and the resurrection. Through such a stirring up of grace, he triggers the soul to set aside all its usual security and look to him for new energy and life.

How might we gain Jesus' help to aid our recovery? How might the one who has lost his childlike sense of spiritual adventure approach our Lord and healer effectively? What is the remedy? We begin by looking to him who is the light of men, and the enlightener of the blind. We are looking for a greater understanding of the condition of our soul. Just to recognise that we have this disease at all is to be half way to spiritual health. The soul that has started to look for Christ's help is beginning to recover already from this sickness and spiritual lethargy. In looking for Jesus Christ concerning this matter, the believer should think of him as God who is able to cause the dead and dry bones to live (see Ezekiel chapter 27). This attitude towards him produces a constant flow of hope, as he sees that his doctor is God himself, for whom nothing is impossible. Caring for what is, after all, a sickness, he should by faith wrap himself up well in the promises of God, and lie down in front of the fire of the Lord, until the heat of his glowing embers thaw out his frozen heart and bring warmth into his cold soul.

If an ongoing pattern of sin has been at the root of the sickness, then repentance and godly sorrow for such evils is the way to bring life back again. We must be sure not to harbour any known sin in the soul, but set ourselves against every known evil as an enemy to our life and recovery.

In all this we must wait with patience, without fretting at God, or arguing with him, if he appears to delay his coming. We must wait with all our humility. Those of us who have sinned our lives away through our own folly are hardly in a place to argue with God when his healing is not instantly received.

We must be cautious about giving way to anything which might perpetuate or increase this deadness of our spirit of kingdom adventure. We must particularly avoid hardness towards others while walking with them. We must be aware of the devil prowling around, and we must not be negligent or careless with the Word of God. Especially, we must be careful not to sadden the Spirit by turning our backs on the things of the kingdom when we begin to glimpse them again.

The seeker needs also to beware of wanting ministry when the

CAN THE LIFE HELP US TO MOVE ON?

kingdom is beginning to be found. It was not for the prodigal to seek a new depth of patronage, having single-handedly destroyed the first one he was granted, he knew it would have been sufficient for him to be made a servant in the house.

What can someone do who is not aware of the weakness discussed in this chapter? Even if there is no real feeling for this spiritual condition, there may be a suspicion lingering that all is not right. If this is the case, the soul must first look to Christ to reveal the probable cause. When you are given even the smallest inkling of your condition from Jesus, who is the Life, then you should ask him to continue to work on your heart.

But how can someone gather up enough faith and trust in the Lord to want to move forward again? If that soul is in denial of anything being wrong, then there will be no desire to move at all. In this weakened state there might not be sufficient strength of faith to overcome the inertia caused by the spiritual sickness itself. Yet even while the soul is in this poor condition it can at least act in a weak and a sickly level of trust in Jesus as leader. The dead Lazarus did not even have that. His family needed to bring Jesus, the resurrection life, to him. How often the prayer of others, or the faithful witness of a believer who is operating in the life of the kingdom, can make a huge difference to the situation. Under the guidance of the Holy Spirit, the kingdom seeker must bring the life of the kingdom to others, and draw them back to the one who is the life.

14

WHEN KINGDOM WORK SEEMS TO BE FADING

Having sought the kingdom for a while, the seeker will see miracle working as a more acceptable everyday event. The great power of what was achieved on Calvary, the power of the message of the cross, now comes more to the fore. *For the message of the cross is foolishness to those who are perishing, but to us who are being saved it is the power of God* (1 Corinthians 1:18).

Before setting out on the kingdom journey the seeker will have been pleasantly surprised when divine healing takes place. Now he is in a place where he will be disappointed, if not dumbfounded, when it does not. Other forms of miracle working that he may never even have considered as possible become thrilling and everyday adventures into the grace of God. Before setting out to seek the kingdom the believer will have understood his duty to the church as being one of supporting it in every way that his talents suggest. Now he sees his duty as gaining knowledge of the Father through Jesus, growing in obedience to him, proclaiming the good news of salvation through Jesus Christ, and healing the sick. Before setting eyes on the kingdom, the minister will have seen it as his duty to help those who suffer; but now he knows that he is commanded to put their situation right through his best attempts at kingdom working. When we do what is commanded of us because it is commanded of us, then we truly become servants of God and the disciples of Christ.

Going on being filled with the Holy Spirit, the seeker will have been well used to enjoying reading scripture at a 'born again' level of interest; now there will be an even greater desire to hear, read and learn ever more from God's written Word.

Before becoming a seeker he will have taken time out from worldly concerns and activities and praised God for his goodness; now he steps back from the kingdom from time to time to attend to secular affairs. This is not to suggest that busy people cannot live in the kingdom; it is to suggest the opposite, namely that even the lives of busy people can indeed be lived in the kingdom. The kingdom of God is within you, regardless of circumstances. Now, when the kingdom seeker finds joy in life, it is not from anything other than the deep assurance that Christ has made his home in him. Sometimes the seeker will be borne upwards on such a cloud of joy that he will be unable to contain it. And why not? We can begin now to grasp something of what Jesus meant as he unveiled a great truth about kingdom living: *"Consider how the lilies grow. They do not labour or spin. Yet I tell you, not even Solomon in all his splendour was dressed like one of these. If that is how God clothes the grass of the field, which is here today, and tomorrow is thrown into the fire, how much more will he clothe you, O you of little faith! And do not set your heart on what you will eat or drink; do not worry about it. For the pagan world runs after all such things, and your Father knows that you need them. But seek his kingdom, and these things will be given to you as well. "Do not be afraid, little flock, for your Father has been pleased to give you the kingdom"* (Luke 12:27–32). That indeed takes us to the very heart of this book's theme. To *seek his kingdom* is what we are to be doing. If we obey this command of the Lord Jesus Christ himself, then he promises that the other things will be given as well. The kingdom is not what we seek as an afterthought, at the end of a list of our life's objectives, it is to be our first objective.

There are times, however, when the believer is under such a

cloud of gloom that he seems to be incapable, unable to discharge any of the commanded duties. Ministry becomes sheer hard work and lifeless — it seems to be dying. The same symptoms can be seen in believers who have not yet really become kingdom seekers; there can be a heaviness about their ministry which needs the same remedy. Christ can help us in this flattened situation, and the seeker can be delivered from under this weight.

We need to consider the various steps and stages of this gloomy situation, something of its origin, its causes and the things that provoke it, and how the Lord brings life once more.

This gloominess comes on by stages. It will be sufficient to mention only the main ones, for example —

1. There might have been a falling back from a high level of watchfulness. When we leave our watchtower we invite Satan to set upon us, as we have pointed out earlier.

2. There are ways of going about our commanded duties, proclaiming the gospel and healing the sick, and there are lazy ways of doing it. We might have been looking for the easiest ways of doing things for a little while (as did the lover in Song of Songs 3:1, when she looked for her beloved on her bed).

3. There may have been a giving way to spiritual drowsiness, a lack of concentration in watching the hand of God. *"I slept"*, says the lover (Song of Songs 5:2f), *"I have taken off my robe – must I put it on again? I have washed my feet – must I soil them again?"* She knew she was not right but, feeling drowsy, she did not shake off that feeling. She took off her coat, washed her feet, and lay down to sleep.

4. There can easily be a contented satisfaction in this drowsy state; it can lead us into believing that our souls are very well when this is not necessarily the case.

5. Even worse, we may be feeling so satisfied and comfortable in this condition that we dismiss any prompting to wake us up. We consider such things to be unloving, and therefore most probably

not from God. In the case of the lover we see the bride turning her heart away and delay in answering the call to her, representing Christ's call to us.

6. It is too easy to defend this condition of the soul, to justify it on the grounds of being secure in places of theological and spiritual development already reached. The lover did the same when she answered the call with the pretext that she had washed her feet and did not want to soil them again.

7. There can even be an angry defence of the situation, especially of a believer's unwillingness to explore the things of the kingdom or to admit that he might not have already done so, or continues to do it anyway. There may be insuperable difficulties mustered in defence of the present way of going about things —rather like the lover protesting that she could not put on her coat again.

8. It may even come to the point that a kingdom calling is completely rejected —like the lover's refusal to get up and open the door.

This is a disastrous condition for the soul to be in. What could cause it? Some, or all, of these things may be considered as having something to do with it—

1. Not bothering to maintain a tender frame of mind, but growing loose in the area of compassion for the poor and for those who are sick, or in suffering of any other kind.

2. Dismissing the Spirit's challenges over the scarcity in ministry of what we may term its commanded duties.

3. To allow the performance of things commanded by God to drift into mere ritual or technique is a sure way to draw a blanket of gloom over any ministry. It can lead to our becoming tired of doing God's will, rather than operating in joyful, willing obedience.

4. This is not such a temptation for believers once they have become kingdom seekers, but when people drown themselves in the cares of the world they create an area of despondency around themselves. Any gospel duties may then be less than

heartily performed, and can be looked on as a burden. Any of the commanded duties of the kingdom may then be set aside on the pretext of lack of time or lack of opportunity. From there the minister begins to neglect or ignore them, and an aversion to them arises through the continuing of that neglect. An unfitness and indisposition for discharging these duties will soon follow.

5. Satan is busy here, driving on this gloom, thickening the cloud with his crafts and wiles, from one stage on to another.

6. On the other hand, it may be that the hand of the sovereign God can be seen at work in the midst of what is happening. He may be ordering matters in his justice and wisdom, to humble those of us who may possibly be puffed up, thinking of ourselves as knowledgeable and experienced enough for any kingdom duty. We might remind ourselves of Peter, who boasted about his own strength, thinking it was nothing to lay down his life for Christ, and to die with him. In the end he could not (or at least did not) speak the truth to a serving girl. We may be receiving a warning to watch and pray, and to work out our own salvation with fear and trembling (see Philippians 2:12) and not to think ourselves above seeking the kingdom.

How then can the light of Jesus Christ indeed be life in the midst of this ministerial dusk?

- Jesus keeps on holding the believer, sometimes keeping life at the root of his ministry even when there may be little outward evidence of any life in the plant.
- He blows on the glowing coal of grace in the soul, in his own time, bringing winter's end and sending a new springtime of life.
- He unties the bands with which the believer was held, enlarging the heart with a desire to go after him, the crucified, risen Lord, to find the kingdom.

WHEN KINGDOM WORK SEEMS TO BE FADING

Now the believer willingly rises up from his bed of security, happily shaking off his drowsiness and former unwillingness; setting about the commanded duties afresh.

The Lord sends gifts of life and strength, helping the soul; he reaches out his hand to touch the sleeper; he touches the heart and wakes the spirit, as he raised the lover up and out of her bed of security and laziness, by putting his hand in at the latch opening. It was then that her heart pounded for him (see Song of Songs 5:4). Able to open the heart (see Revelation 3:7) he can move our hearts to faith again. By getting a lively faith on the move again, he makes the soul strong in the Lord, and in the power of his might, (see Ephesians 6:10). The soul becomes able to run and not be weary, and to walk and not be faint (see Isaiah 40:31).

How might we, with the help of the Lord, overtake or arrest any 'slowing down' of the soul? Given that the believer is in some way aware of this decay, and seriously seeks to be out from under this weight of oppression, he should—

1. Look to Christ for sharper eyesight and insight, to get a clearer picture of the awfulness of his condition. Alarmed and awake, he might then be more willing to use the prescribed means of recovery.

2. Run to the fountain of Jesus' blood to get the guilt of his past sins washed away, and then, reconciled, he will know that the Father's face shines on him.

3. Give a great deal of thanksgiving for the fact that the Holy Spirit can grant the gift of a repentant heart. Pray that your own sorrow for former sinful attitudes will be pointed out gently, thoroughly and in a way that will be heart changing. Pray that Christ would put his hand in, by the latch opening, so that the heart will leap again for him.

4. Look to him as the good Shepherd, strengthening and healing others, including the sick (see Ezekiel 34:16). This will strengthen hope.

5. Lay hold of Christ as his strength, in order that the seeker's feet can be made like those of a deer, and that he can be made capable of walking on high places (see Habakkuk 3:19). He should also hold on tightly to the promise given in Isaiah 41:10, *"So do not fear, for I am with you; do not be dismayed, for I am your God. I will strengthen you and help you; I will uphold you with my righteous right hand."*

6. Having done all this, he should then set out afresh to carry out in the strength of Jesus the things he, the Lord, has commanded, constantly looking to him for help and the supply of gifts. Although the seeker might find that he is not aware of divine assistance as much or as soon as he expected, he should not be discouraged but keep going. When no more can be done, it will be time to offer himself to God again, ready and willing to carry out the kingdom commanded duties, as if the supply of gifts were imminent.

Finally, it will be necessary to be on guard every day against Satan finding a way to pull the seeker back down into the trough.

We need to do these things:

- Carefully watch out for the evils which brought on the gloom in the first place especially lack of tenderness, lack of watchfulness, laziness, fleshly security, formality and lack of seriousness.
- Beware of giving way to moods of despondency, or concluding that the work of the kingdom may be fruitless in your case. This discourages the soul and contradicts God's will.
- Exercise the grace of patient waiting.
- Wait for positive employment in the kingdom. This serves, as it were, to rub the dead and cold limb in front of the fire until it becomes warm again.

WHEN KINGDOM WORK SEEMS TO BE FADING

- Always go on being filled with the Holy Spirit.
- Look to Jesus alone. He promises to send the Holy Spirit, who is the giver of life. Do not fix time limits for his refreshing, renewing, reviving work in you.
- Cherish and stir up with thanksgiving any small beginnings that occur.
- Welcome every movement of the Spirit. In this way the seeker avoids grieving the Spirit of God (see Ephesians 4:30), or putting out his fire (see 1 Thessalonians 5:19). Above all, the seeker should always hold Christ, and everything that is his in the kingdom, to be precious and lovely. This is how we can keep some room in our own heart open for him, until once again we become aware of his living presence with us.

15

CAN LIFE RETURN?

There can be a deadness of ministry and in our attempts to worship when it seems as though the Lord is hiding himself. This may seem especially tragic as the Lord is the seeker's life, and *the fountain of life* (Psalm 36:9), *whose love is better than life* (Psalm 63:3), and whose *anger lasts only a moment, but his favour lasts a lifetime* (Psalm 30:5).

This situation, where a believer can trace his Christian experience back over what seems to be a rough mountain trail of unanswered prayer, is very common. The most common reaction to it is complete denial of the situation, as it is sometimes wrongly thought to be incompatible with the goodness and love of God, reigning in his kingdom. Facing up to the circumstances, however, will bring better results. So let us take a look at the symptoms in the believer of this supposed hiding of the Lord's face; some possible reasons for his seeming to do so; how Christ can resuscitate the situation; and how the seeker should handle this matter in a way which is conducive to healing.

As to the first of these, here are some of the more common symptoms.

1. Believers do not often complain aloud about God's 'hiding', they store it up in the bottom of their souls. Down there may be heard the cry, *"My God, my God, why have you forsaken me?"* (Psalm 22:1); and, *Look on me and answer, O LORD my God* (Psalm 13:3).

2. They long for a glimpse of his face, a wave of his hand, but do not get it because he seems to be hiding from them. (See Psalm 13:1.) The lover searched for quite a while. (See Song of Songs 5, and Psalm 22:1f, in this same context.)

3. They look for a way out of this prayer trough, and, not finding one, things seem worse. *Hope deferred makes the heart sick, but a longing fulfilled is a tree of life* (Proverbs 13:12).

4. The whole business of unanswered prayer is a mystery to them. *How long, O Lord? Will you forget me forever? How long will you hide your face from me?* (Psalm 13:1). They cannot understand why it is that God appears to them to have become deaf to their prayers.

5. The better experience of others seems to bring little comfort, and again the words of the psalmist bring us to the authentic feeling: *In you our fathers put their trust; they trusted and you delivered them. They cried to you and were saved; in you they trusted and were not disappointed. But I am a worm and not a man, scorned by men and despised by the people* (Psalm 22:4–6). The writer's forebears were taken care of by God, but that fact brought him no peace of mind; he adds, straight away, in verse 6, *But I am a worm and not a man, scorned by men and despised by the people. Yet you are enthroned as the Holy One; you are the praise of Israel.*

6. Even when the believer can look back and see God's hand being fruitful in the way that his earlier life was ordered, he might still complain at the lack of attention he thinks God is showing him.

If anyone should ask why the Lord should deal with his own people in this way, we remind ourselves at once that everything he does is wise and holy. All his ways are perfect. He does not make any mistakes. Possible reasons are suggested here:

1. In order to correct a tendency to complacency as depicted in the lover of Song of Songs 5:6f.

2. In order to discipline the seeker for ill-use of previously entrusted gifts and talents (see Matthew 25:28).

3. In order to prove whether the seeker's carrying out of the commanded duties has been pure and righteous, containing no other motive than that of obedience itself. If it is, then the soul will be pressed on to obey without any encouragement.

4. In order to exercise and test our faith, patience, hope and compassion (see Psalm 13:5f and God's response in Psalm 22:24).

5. In order to check as to whether the believer is putting his security and self confidence elsewhere. He did this to David. See Psalm 30:6–8, when he said that his mountain stood strong, and that he would never be moved. It then seemed to David that the Lord hid his face from him, and he was deeply troubled by it.

6. In order to wake believers up and out of their slumber of security, starting them off again with a more diligent and enthusiastic obedience to commanded duty, as we can see depicted in the lover of Song of Songs 5.

7. In order to sharpen the seeker's pangs of hunger for him and the things of his kingdom.

Any or all of these reasons are possible. Then how can Christ resuscitate the situation?

1. By taking away, because of the seeker's repentance, the sinful causes of this apparent distance that seems to have grown back between the believer and God. Jesus has laid down his life and shed his blood for the remission of sins, to make provision for the removal of those sins from our lives.

2. Jesus can give deliverance from the situation.

3. He keeps the cold soul alive on such a winter's day by continually breathing into it.

4. He holds up the flagging soul, imparting gifts. (See Matthew 15:5.)

5. By setting the soul to work with the Spirit's own medicine: leading us to cry 'Abba, Father', to plead, to long, to wait. These are heart-reviving medicines to the true kingdom seeker.

6. By teaching the soul a lesson: to submit to everything that God does. This will encourage the seeker to acknowledge his righteousness, his greatness and his sovereignty.

7. By drawing back the veil, when he feels the time is right again, he fills the soul with joy in the light of God's countenance. This will cause it to sing once more.

Lastly, we should consider how the seeker should handle this healing.

1. He should humble himself under God. There is no arguing with the Lord. *'As surely as I live,' says the Lord, 'every knee will bow before me; every tongue will confess to God'* (Romans 14:11).

2. He should confirm God in everything and say with David in Psalm 22:3, *Yet you are enthroned as the Holy One; you are the praise of Israel.*

3. He should see himself as the least among his friends and colleagues in the faith. *'I am a worm,'* said David, Psalm 22:6, *'and not a man.'*

4. He should look to find his own case in the symptoms listed here, then he should run away with them to the fountain, the blood of Christ, so that they can be purged. His conscience can be sprinkled from a dead life (see Exodus 24:8), and his soul washed in the fountain that has been made available for the washing away of sin (see Hebrews 9:19 and 10:22.)

5. He must be praying for the Holy Spirit's guidance and help to discover other unknown acts or thoughts which may have grieved the Spirit. *"Suppose a man says to God, 'I am guilty but will offend no more. Teach me what I cannot see; if I have done wrong, I will not do so again.'"* This was Elihu's advice to Job, quoted in chapter 34:31f.

6. Hold on firmly to Christ, and rest there with satisfaction and joy. Hold on fast, and ride out the storm in the dark night.

7. The seeker should remain open to opportunities to commend God highly to others. This follows the example of the lover

depicted in Song of Songs 5:10–16.

8. He should collect himself up and throw himself back into the business of seeking. The lover of Song of Songs 5:6 did so. The discouragement meted out to her by the watchmen did not put her off.

9. The seeker must be careful to ensure that any revival of his spiritual life is centred on Jesus Christ, as the Father will not be seen through anyone or anything else.

But someone will always ask: what if, after all this, the situation continues and very few prayers and pleas to heaven seem to elicit a response? The answer is that life is one thing, and comfort is another. Grace is one thing, and a warm glimpse of God's face is another. The one is vital life to the seeker, the other is not, but only comforting. During this time the seeker should go on being faithful to God, even though he might miss being comforted for a while. In time, what will be discovered is that, in truth, life has never been absent, for believers are a temple of the Holy Spirit, and Jesus entered in when we first received him. Thus the living divine presence, which first made the believer a new creation at the new birth, continues and is active in the believer whether we are aware of that or sense any effects or not. The problem may well be that we have not yet learnt to operate by faith rather than sight.

Part Four
NO ONE COMES TO THE FATHER EXCEPT....

16

OUR FATHER IN HEAVEN... YOUR KINGDOM COME

Finally, we can set down some key points about the kingdom of God, for emphasis and clarification.

The kingdom belongs to the Father, and the crucified Christ is its King. What was won on Calvary hangs in the air, so to speak, in the kingdom, and therefore the atmosphere of it is restorative. The one who repents and believes dies with Christ and is raised with him; the significance of this is worked out on the seeker's way along the road of sanctification towards the heart of the kingdom. The nearer he gets to the centre of the kingdom, the more the seeker realises the significance of the fact that he is buried in Christ's death and has been raised with Christ. The seeker becomes immersed more and more in the resurrection life and the restoration work of the kingdom. He begins to receive more from the Lord, as the old Adam moves out and the new Adam (Jesus) moves in. When it is brought near to a needy soul, the kingdom can heal, save and deliver that soul from everything that can oppress it in any area of life, because only the will of God can subsist in the kingdom. (See Luke 4:18f.) *"But if I drive out demons by the finger of God, then the kingdom of God has come to you"* (Luke 11:20).

The kingdom is not only a place full of people being saved and healed; it is full of a crucified Christ who reflects the will of the Father to heal. It is essential for the seeker to be absolutely clear about this fundamental point concerning the character of the kingdom. It only exists in and through Jesus Christ, because — and here is the whole marrow of the gospel — our healing and salvation hinge on it, for he is 'the chief cornerstone'. (See Isaiah 38:16, 1 Peter 1:5f.) He is the only safe, solid and true peace and source of comfort. A mistake about that would be extremely dangerous, putting all our future in jeopardy.

This restorative truth is a major area in which Satan attacks. He raises up errors, false opinions and heresies, causing numbers of teachers to be confused and to raise up grave doubts in the congregation of the Lord, hindering folk from receiving all the benefits that Christ has won for them. Single-minded faithful believing is so essential for the believer, for . . . *when he asks, he must believe and not doubt, because he who doubts is like a wave of the sea, blown and tossed by the wind. That man should not think he will receive anything from the Lord* (James 1:6f).

Our naturally corrupt human hearts would rather find any other way to the kingdom. Anything and everything will be easily absorbed into the mind so long as it is an alternative to the truth about the way to the kingdom. There is a multitude of wrong ways presented to the seeker, some of which have been mentioned in these pages. All this should make it very clear to us that we must keep our desires focused in order to break through into a working acquaintance with the kingdom, to make sure that we are in it, to hold it fast and to keep it pure in our life and the performance of our commanded duty.

There are many strongholds set against knowledge of the kingdom, and especially against the knowledge of how to seek it. We need to consider these. Firstly, there is the belief that what has been learned before must be the only true basis for testing heresy. The seeker, however, demolishes consequential arguments by taking hold of them and comparing them to the truth about Jesus as revealed in the New Testament. We sometimes have to do battle for the truths of the kingdom. Paul wrote: *I beg you that when I come I may not have to be as bold as I expect to be toward some people who think that we live by the standards of this world. For though we live in the world, we do not wage war as the world does. The weapons we fight with are not the weapons of the world. On the contrary, they have divine power to demolish strongholds. We demolish arguments and every pretension that sets itself up against the knowledge of God, and we take captive every thought to make it obedient to Christ* (2 Corinthians 10:2–5).

Secondly, there is the mistaken belief that church, Christendom and the kingdom are identical. What we have seen in so many passages of scripture is that they are distinct.

Thirdly, there is the way in which many are encouraged not to expect anything much from God, in order to avoid the possibility of disappointment. This has the appearance of pastoral care, but it actually derives from a mixture of 'negative faith' and fear of loss of self-esteem.

All this means that it can be far from easy to have this way accepted — that the kingdom is the place in which God's will is being done, and that the way to it is not through argument and learning but by following the way, the truth and the life. The seriousness of this matter dictates that we emphasise these things:

- Nature, or any other religion or spiritual opinion, will not teach this way; Jesus is the *only* way to the Father, the only Saviour.
- Our *natural* human inclination is to fight against God's way.
- The way into the kingdom given to us by Jesus runs against our haughty pride and innate sense of self-importance.

- We can see from all this the Christian's first lesson: to learn to deny himself.

It is hoped that all these thoughts will serve to humble us, making us jealous about safeguarding our own hearts and patterns of thinking. The seeker, having entered through the gate of justification on his knees (see Matthew 19:24), and having begun the walk along the sanctifying road, has all hope and strength built on Jesus Christ, and on nothing and no-one else. Ups and downs, differing levels of a sense of peace and joy, do not come with secular or church gains but according to how close or far away the seeker feels to him. The concrete security of childhood begins to return through the seeker's leaning towards Jesus —resting on him alone, expecting ready access, acceptance and a hearing. He will quickly develop a deep assurance, in the face of all temptation and worry, that Christ is his way to the kingdom and that he is the safest of roads to travel on.

Even the most ardent seekers need to be regularly reminded of everything in this book because Satan is busy trying to pull seekers off this road, persuading them to sit down on the verge and rest. Moreover, the seeker's own bias towards sin, as we described it earlier (the 'flesh'), the evil heart of unbelief, is always drawing him off the way. Because of the negative influences of the world, the flesh and the devil, the seeker is often tempted to give up under pressures of many different kinds. When things are going well, the seeker feels encouraged to keep all his mind and heart focused on kingdom business. Kingdom people may frequently be seen as the spiritual enemies of dry formalism. Critics will attempt, through careless criticism and backbiting, to knock the traveller off his feet.

All this shows the need for two things: the seeker's continuing humility, and the need to be continually preaching the good news of salvation through Jesus Christ crucified and risen, the call to repentance and faith in him alone.

The seeker's heart will begin to break. He will discover another truth along the way, that there are not as many believers as he had previously supposed. No one comes to the Father except through Jesus; and few people seem to know the true way of employing and applying the grace of the King and the kingdom to their own lives and to the lives of those around them. Of all who have had preached to them Jesus, who is the way, the truth and the life, how few believe, follow and practice the truth.

Here is the greatest gift of all: in and through Jesus alone we can find these things:

- Knowledge of the Father. *"All things have been committed to me by my Father. No one knows the Son except the Father, and no one knows the Father except the Son and those to whom the Son chooses to reveal him"* (Matthew 11:27).
- Friendship with Jesus. *You are my friends if you do what I command you.*
- The door to the kingdom on earth. He is the door (see John 10:1–4).
- He is the door to life in the hereafter. Jesus has gone before us and prepared a place for those who are his.
- The way to communicate with the Father. (See John 16:23, Revelation 8:3); in thanksgiving (see Romans 1:8, Colossians 3:17); and in praise (see Hebrews 13:15; Ephesians 3:21).
- It is only because of him that we have an open door to the Father. (See Ephesians 2:18, 3:21 and Hebrews 4:16).

How are we to make use of the kingdom? How does the seeker do what he can to ensure that other believers enjoy kingdom blessings that are available to those who are in Christ?

Firstly, the seeker should always be mindful that kingdom benefits are to be asked for. Every benefit of Calvary listed in these pages is available to the penitent, believing supplicant who comes to Christ and *asks* him in all humility. Consider these benefits

which flow from the finished work of Jesus on the cross:
- Peace. (See Isaiah 53:4f; Ephesians 2:13f.)
- Abundance. (See 2 Corinthians 8:9 and 2 Corinthians 9:8, and consider that the curse in Deuteronomy 28:15, and in Deuteronomy 28:47f, has been lifted.)
- Eternal life. (See Hebrews 2:9 and John 3:16.)
- A new nature. (See Romans 6:6.)
- Healing. (See Isaiah 53:5.)
- Righteousness. (See 2 Corinthians 5:21.)

This is why the atmosphere in the kingdom is described as being restorative. All these benefits are there to be breathed in, lived, and enjoyed by believers.

Secondly, the seeker will be overcome with the heartfelt longing to impart these gifts. However, they are not the seeker's own gifts to dispose of, they are the gifts of the King to those who approach him in repentance and trusting, child-like expectant faith and humbly seek them from him, trusting only in his one sacrifice on the cross for the forgiveness of sins. But every Christian has a mandate to witness, and should always be ready to speak the word of truth, the good news. Remember that Jesus allowed people to choose whether to receive him. Each person could come to him in penitence and faith or, tragically, reject him.

Be encouraged — as you go on repenting whenever the Spirit prompts you; as you go on believing in Jesus; as you go on living in him, who is the risen one, persevering, overcoming all the assaults of the enemy, rejoicing in the hope that God has given in his Word.